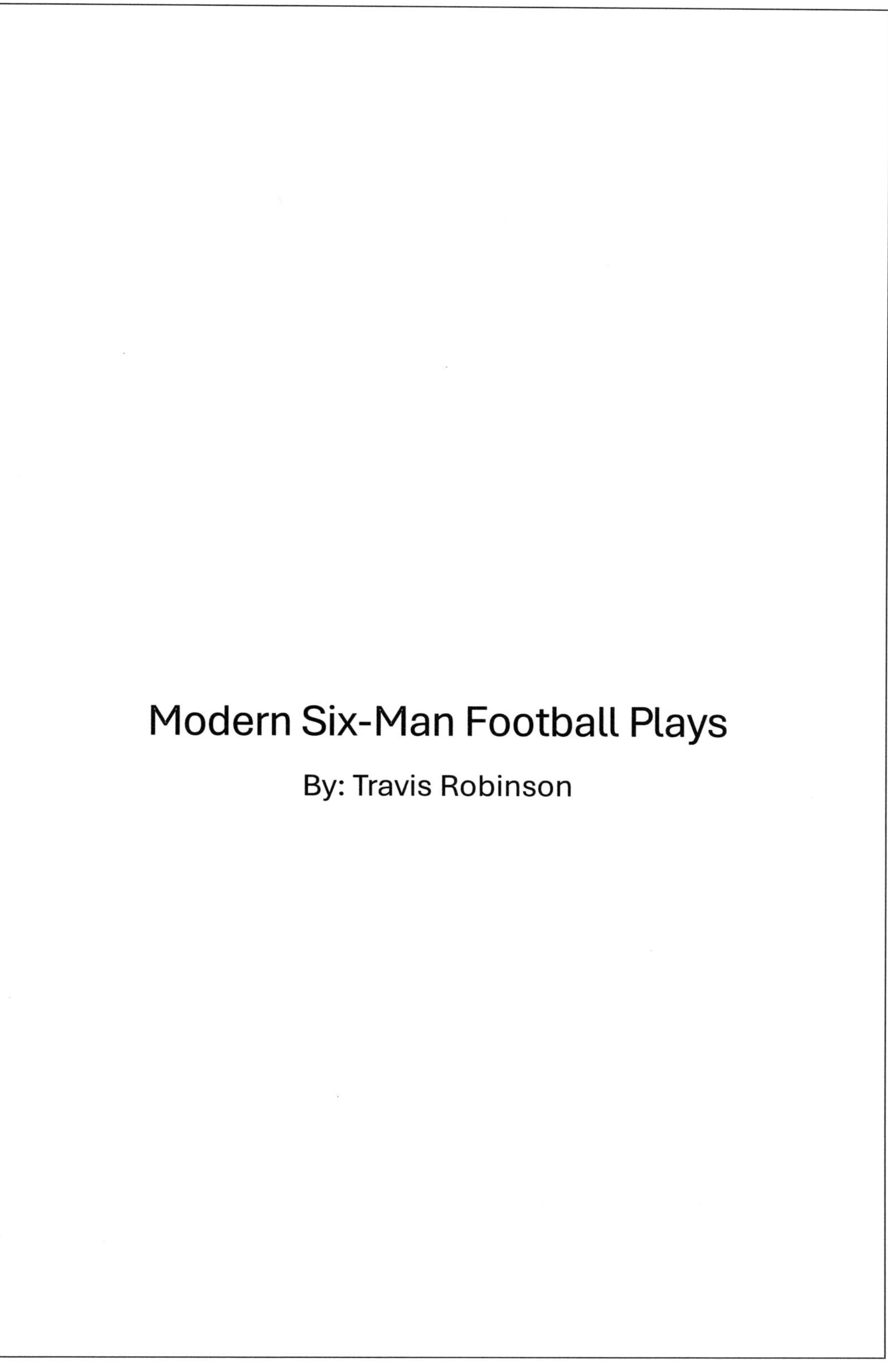

# Modern Six-Man Football Plays

By: Travis Robinson

*To the one I truly do this for, and everything He has done for me. Thank you, God, for helping me follow your lead. "FOR HIM!"*

*To my beautiful Daughter Blaire, thank you for making every day the happiest day of my life. Continue your joy and keep dreaming big.*

*To my amazing wife Aime, thank you for continuing to Coach the Coach. Thank you for being the best mother & Wife, and most of all for always pushing me on my dreams.*

*To the FBCA Coaching Staff, thank you for taking a chance on me, and teaching me what it truly means to be humble.*

"Creativity is an evolutionary process of refinement"

-Pablo Picasso

## Table of Contents

# Introduction

In Small Towns with populations barely pushing 1,000 people, a high school is made up of no more than 100 kids. These towns play a beautiful game called Six-Man football. We all watch the "Main event" on Saturday's and Sunday's, and most of you reading this book grew up playing what you know as 11-man football, the most traditional way to play it. I also played 11-man for all my high school career...until my senior year. Growing up as a Texas kid, 6-man football was something I never knew even existed.

When I was younger, it was decided that I would be homeschooled, so when my family decided to move to Colorado, there were no laws against Homeschoolers playing with any school they'd like. But when my family moved back to Texas for my Senior year, this indeed was not the case, and I had to find a homeschool organization to play with...thus lead to my introduction of six-man football.

For anyone that has experienced this game for the first time, whether it be a fan, player, or a coach, it can feel quite confusing and overwhelming to adapt to, especially when you have been used to one style of the game your whole life. But there's something about seeing that first game, the first time ever witnessing "Basketball on grass," if you open your mind to it, and dedicate yourself to this game it can be the game you never knew you loved.

I have spent the last few months diving through and studying all the film I can get my hands on from the past five years and wanted to share everything I could to help spread the much-needed resources in the Six-man community.

If you are brand new to Six-Man or have been around the game for over 20 years. I hope that this book gives you something that you can take away from it and help grow your knowledge of the game whether that be as a Coach, parent, player, or fan!

# Six-Man Rules Refresher

I wanted to make sure that I overviewed the differences between 6-man and 11-man. Especially for those who are picking this book up and are brand new to the Six-man world.

It is my belief, that these rule differences are what truly causes 6-man football to be the most creative driven sport today. Here are the main 6-man rules you should know.

**The Field**

A typical 6-man field is 80 Yards long and 40 Yards wide. Compared to an 11-man field that is 100 x 53 1/3 yards. It is common to see for teams who still have 11-man fields, that they will "tape off" their sidelines to fit the 6-man field dimensions. But there are plenty of schools who have had custom fields made just for 6-man! (See Below)

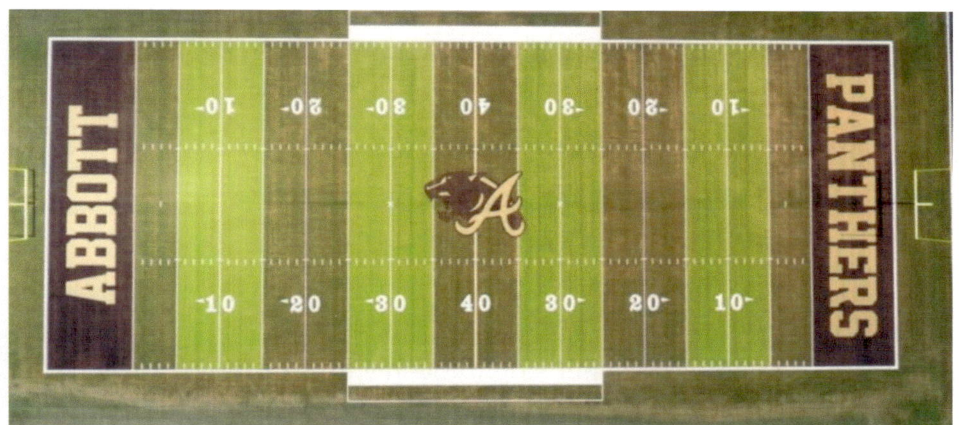


*Abbott panther Stadium; www.abottisd.org*

**Getting "45ed"**

A Common term you will hear a lot throughout the 6-man football world is "We 45ed them" or unfortunately "We got 45ed." To put it in more simple terms, this is simply a mercy rule put in place for 6-man games. This rule was put into place since the scoring tends to be so high.

If at halftime, or anytime after the second half begins, if a team leads by 45 points or more, the game is over. (For example: If Team A is up 44-0 at halftime, the game will continue unless Team A scores again.)

In the State of Texas at least, 6-man football is the only level that uses any kind of mercy rule.

**The 15 Yard Mark**

Another yardage rule is that instead of your typical 10 yards to get a first down, it is now 15 yards to get a first down. But it's not quite Canadian football! We still use four downs for the opportunity to convert.

This same 15 Yard measuring stick is also used on kickoffs. As in the ball is not "Live" till it reaches that 15-yard threshold.

It is also very common in 6-man for teams to mainly onside kick throughout a game.

**Every Receiver is Eligible**

It's as simple as it sounds! All 6 of your offensive weapons are eligible to receive or run the ball. That's right, even your Center! In 6-Man, you will never see a "ineligible man downfield" penalty called.

## Scoring

A Touchdown is still worth the same in 6-man football, the good ole 6-points! It is extra points & field goals that are changed. With only 4 players able to block on a PAT or Field Goal, it can be a very hard task to complete, since the rush is so much quicker than that in 11-man.

A PAT by no means is "automatic" in 6-man. So compared to 11-man, the points are reversed. Making a kicked PAT is 2 points, and just running or passing the ball in the endzone is 1 point.

Although rare, a Scrimmaged Field Goal is worth 4 points instead of 3.

**Top 5 highest Scoring 6-Man games of all time.**

| 1 | 2024 | Bellville Faith | 148 | Waco Valor Prep | 112 |
|---|---|---|---|---|---|
| 2 | 2017 | Campbell | 125 | Fannindel | 122 |
| 3 | 2024 | Waco Valor Prep | 146 | Midland Holy Cross | 99 |
| 4 | 2011 | S.A The Winston | 122 | S.A Town East | 120 |
| 5 | 2011 | Fort Davis | 124 | Midland Trinty | 108 |

*SixManFootball.com. (2025). Highest scoring games. https://sixmanfootball.com/scores/highest-scoring-games*

## The Exchange Rule

Out of all the rules that we've broken down, this will be the most important one for you to know! When advancing the ball on offense, there must be a "Clean exchange" before the ball can go past the Line of scrimmage. So, what does this mean?

For example, after your Quarterback takes the snap from the center, he cannot just take the snap and run at this point (R.I.P the Tush Push).

But what he can do is either pitch, handoff, or pass the ball forward past the Line of scrimmage.

This rule is where the true creativity of 6-man comes into play. A way a lot of coaches get around this rule commonly, is by either using the Quarterback or what's referred to as an "Up-back" and have them pitch back to their best athlete, so they are now eligible to either throw or run.

*Follet executing a "clean exchange"; Texas 1A Fan; 2024*

# Common 6-Man Formations

Before we jump into the good stuff, I wanted to drop a quick overview of some of the more popular sets in 6-man football.

Typically, most 6-man coaches will categorize offensive systems into three different categories. Tight, Hybrid, and Spread. I will be separating this book into these three sections and will go more into depth before each one to understand what makes them so different.

For now, here are (in my opinion), the most popular formations in each category!

## Tight Sets

**<u>The "T" Set</u>**

Top Teams that run this set:

| | | |
|---|---|---|
|   |   |   |

**J-Bird**

Top Teams that run this set:

| | | |
|---|---|---|
|  |  |  |

## Hybrid Sets

**Bullet**

Top Teams that run this set:

| | | |
|---|---|---|
|  |  |  |

**J-Gun**

Top Teams that run this set:

| | | |
|---|---|---|
|  |  |  |

# Spread Sets

## Diamond

Top Teams that run this set:

| | | |
|---|---|---|
|  |  |  |

**Ruby (3 WR's)**

Top Teams that run this set:

No matter the set you decide to run & make a staple of your offensive system, know that the most important aspect is knowing what fits your personal. And while this may sound like a coaching cliché, this can be one of the most important things you consider before deciding what to install for your athletes.

To use a Chess analogy, not every piece can move anywhere on the board like a Queen can, and our pawns can only move one square at a time but sometimes can help us finally knock down that king.

Every piece on our board matters, but where we fit those pieces is a crucial part to a successful system. Especially in 6-man where your best athletes can truly shine.

# QR Codes

Throughout the book you will see something on the top left of every play included. These are QR codes (Like you see here.)

*SixManFootball.com*

So, what are these for exactly? Glad you asked! With every play included, also comes a film clip! This is by far my favorite part of this project. You can scan any of the QR codes in this book, and the film clip will match the play you are looking at!

**How do you scan a QR Code?**

If you're new to the QR code game that's fine! All you need is your smartphone or tablet.

1. Open the camera app on your device.
2. Hold your camera over the QR code to scan it.

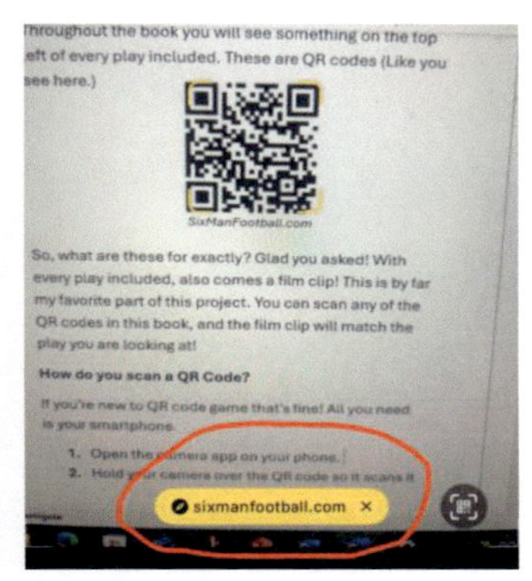


3. A link should pop up, click it!
4. Ta-Da! You are now watching film.

**Bonus!** Gold QR Codes can have up to 50+ film clips!

# The Last Six 6-Man State Championships

I wanted to make sure that I included a detail that I believe is an important topic in the debate of the 3 offensive systems (Tight, Hybrid, Spread). I figured It could be very helpful to show previous state championships and what style of offenses those teams ran.

Whatever you take from this information, know that there will never be a perfect system. You will always install what's perfect for your kids.

At the end of the day, keep it simple!

"The ability to simplify means to eliminate the unnecessary, so that that the necessary may speak."

-Hans Hofman

### UIL – Last Six State Championships

| Year | Div. | Team | ***Set*** | PTS | Team | ***Set*** | PTS |
|---|---|---|---|---|---|---|---|
| 2019 | 1 | Blum | ***Tight*** | 58 | Mclean | ***Tight*** | 52 |
| 2019 | 2 | Richland Springs | ***Tight*** | 62 | Motley County | ***Tight*** | 16 |
| 2020 | 1 | Sterling City | ***Tight*** | 68 | May | ***Tight*** | 22 |
| 2020 | 2 | Balmorhea | ***Tight*** | 74 | Richland Springs | ***Tight*** | 38 |
| 2021 | 1 | Westbrook | ***Tight*** | 72 | May | ***Tight*** | 66 |
| 2021 | 2 | Strawn | ***Tight*** | 73 | Motley County | ***Tight*** | 28 |
| 2022 | 1 | Benjamin | ***Tight*** | 68 | Loraine | ***Hybrid*** | 20 |
| 2022 | 2 | Westbrook | ***Tight*** | 69 | Abbott | ***Tight*** | 24 |
| 2023 | 1 | Gordon | ***Tig/Hy*** | 70 | Westbrook | ***Hybrid*** | 10 |
| 2023 | 2 | Benjamin | ***Tight*** | 82 | Oglesby | ***Hybrid*** | 34 |
| 2024 | 1 | Gordon | ***Tig/Hy*** | 70 | Whiteface | ***Tight*** | 24 |
| 2024 | 2 | Jayton | ***Tight*** | 54 | Oakwood | ***Tig/Hy*** | 8 |

*Jayton after winning the UIL 1A-D2 State Championship; Texas 1A fan; 2024*

# Tight

The simplest way to define a Tight offense is by the Quarterback being under center. It also means that we will usually always see less than 1 Wide Receiver included in the formation. The typical mindset of a Tight offensive system is to be run first and usually includes some sort of sweep as its main bread & butter play.

**Blocking Rules**

Every system needs base blocking rules, it's important to know that not everyone teaches blocking the same way, there are always many ways to skin a cat!

For this book, we will use the verbiage that's commonly known as **G.O.D** blocking rules. Which stands for Gap-On–Downfield. There are many ways to word these assignments; "Down-Head up-Backer, Gap-On-Over-Backside." The list goes on. View these rules as a base ground layer for your players, it is essentially a giant checklist they go through before the ball is snapped.

## Gap

The first question a lineman should ask himself is "Is there a defender in my Gap?" If that answer is yes, then we block him! In most coaching community's this is considered a "down block."

But what exactly does it mean for someone "to be in my gap?"

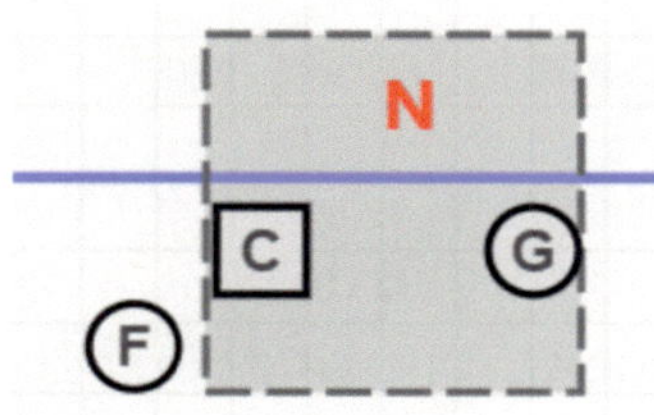


Let's say that we have a run play going to the **RIGHT.** Well, when using G.O.D rules we assume that all of our blocking rules start opposite of the play direction. So, when going through our blocking checklist we check in the gap to our **LEFT** first and either decide if that is who we are blocking or move on in our checklist.

## On

Is there anyone in my Gap? No? Then we move onto our second rule. Is anyone Head up directly on me? Yes.

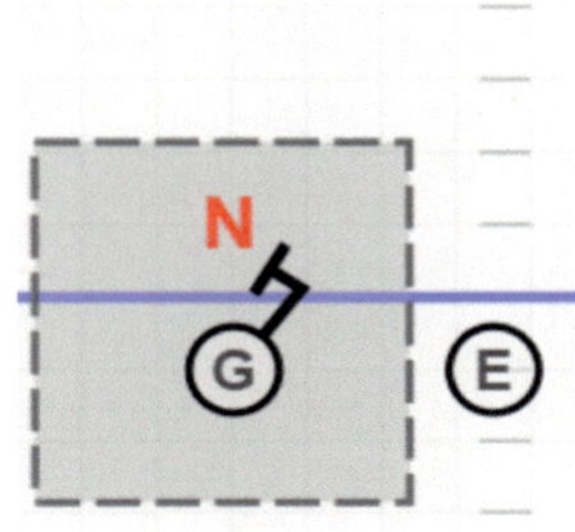


Then we will block the defender head up on us. Our first step on a "On" block is much different than what it would be on a gap block. When we are performing a base gap block – our 1st step would be opposite of the direction where the play is going. (So, the left foot if the play is going right.) But when executing a "On" block this can almost be considered a "Zone" block, because any first step that is TOWARDS the play is seen as a Zone block. (If the play is going Right, then our first step is with our right foot.) When no one is in our gap, and no one is head up on us, then we move on in our checklist.

## Downfield (2nd Level)

The last item on our checklist is to get to the 2nd level and likely block a Linebacker.

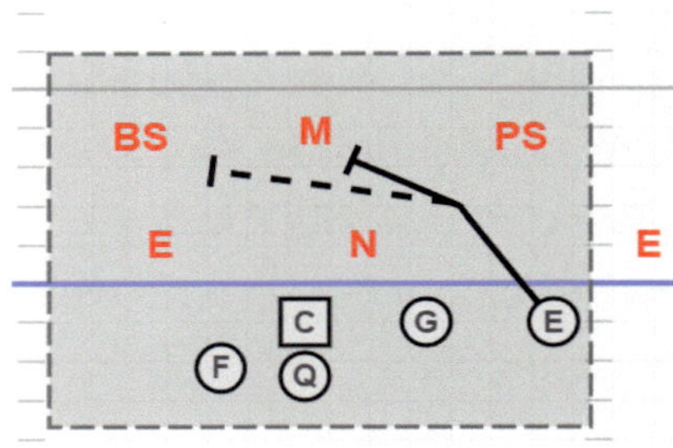


But what LB do we block? This varies on a lot of different coaching styles, but also the scheme itself. You can have them block the Mike (Middle of the field), the Backside LB, or the Playside LB.

Extra Page for Notes & Diagrams

Extra Page for Notes & Diagrams

# The Famous T Sweep

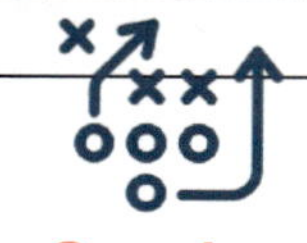

| Set: | T | Team: | Westbrook |
|---|---|---|---|
| Play: | Sweep | Scheme: | Gap |

**Coaches Corner**

The RB's alignment in most T sets – especially for Sweep is very close to the LOS @ 4-5 Yards!

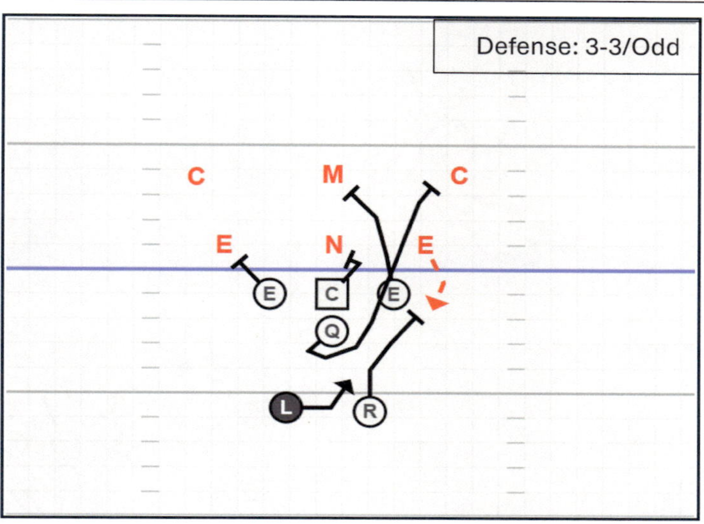


| C: | "On" Rules - Seal | QB: | Pitch – 2nd Level |
|---|---|---|---|
| PSTE: | 2nd Level | LHB: | Sidestep – Get Downhill |
| BSTE: | Down/Backside | RHB: | Kickout PSDE |

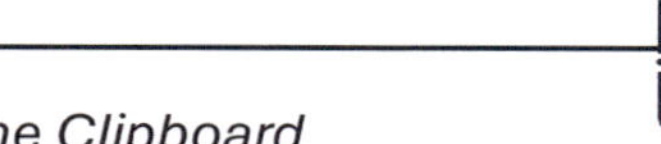

*The Clipboard*

One could argue that this is the most run play in all of 6-man. The idea here is to get downhill as FAST as possible, and you are putting every single body you have possible on a defender! Most teams that run this scheme use base G.O.D blocking rules. But any "On" block is considered a "Zone Block", since our first step is TOWARDS the playside direction. For you 11-man old-school guys, this play reminds me a lot of the old "Double wing – Super Power!"

# More Variations

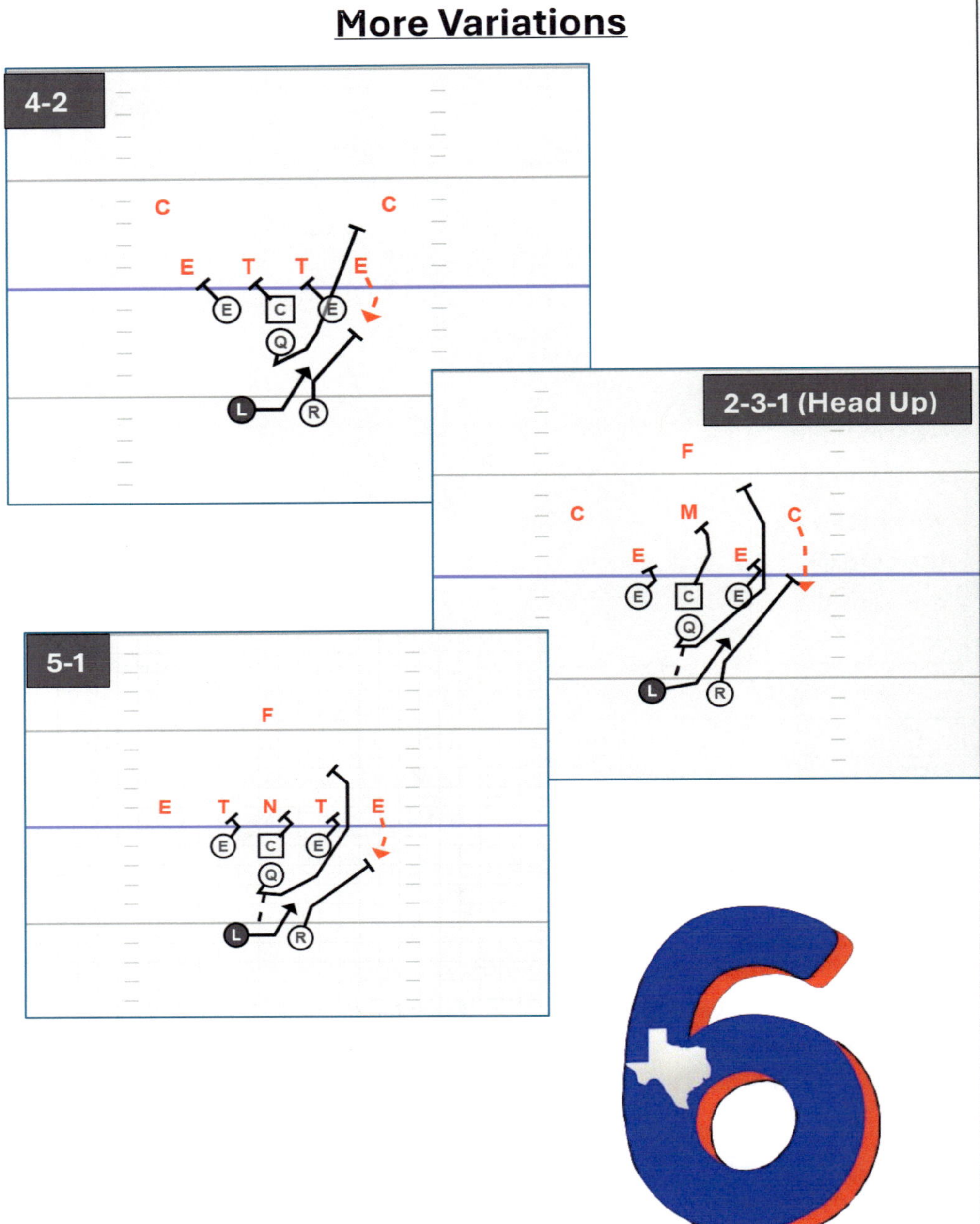

## Abbott's Weak Sweep

| **Set:** | J-Bird | **Team:** | Abbott |
|---|---|---|---|
| **Play:** | Sweep | **Scheme:** | Gap/Zone |

### *Coaches Corner*

The Abbott system is known to have built in audibles for over-aggressive defenses (Like shown here)

Defense: 3-3 Strong (Walked-up Mike)

| **C:** | On/Cut | **QB:** | Pitch w/Open hand – 2nd Level |
|---|---|---|---|
| **G:** | 2nd Level | **FB:** | (Read PSDE) Seal or Kick Out |
| **TE:** | 2nd Level | **RB:** | 1 Sidestep – Read FB's Block |

*The Clipboard*

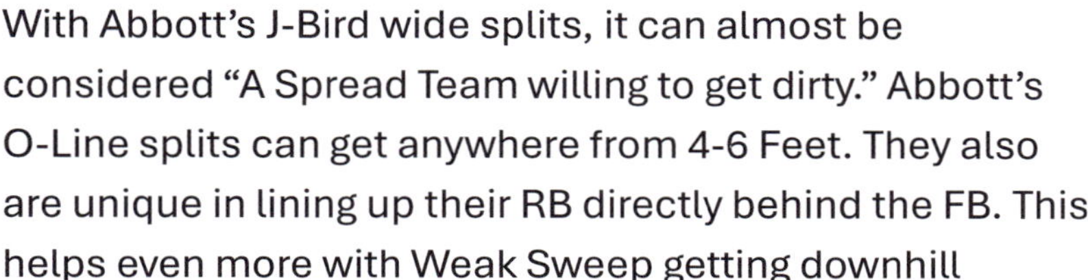

With Abbott's J-Bird wide splits, it can almost be considered "A Spread Team willing to get dirty." Abbott's O-Line splits can get anywhere from 4-6 Feet. They also are unique in lining up their RB directly behind the FB. This helps even more with Weak Sweep getting downhill quicker.

# More Variations

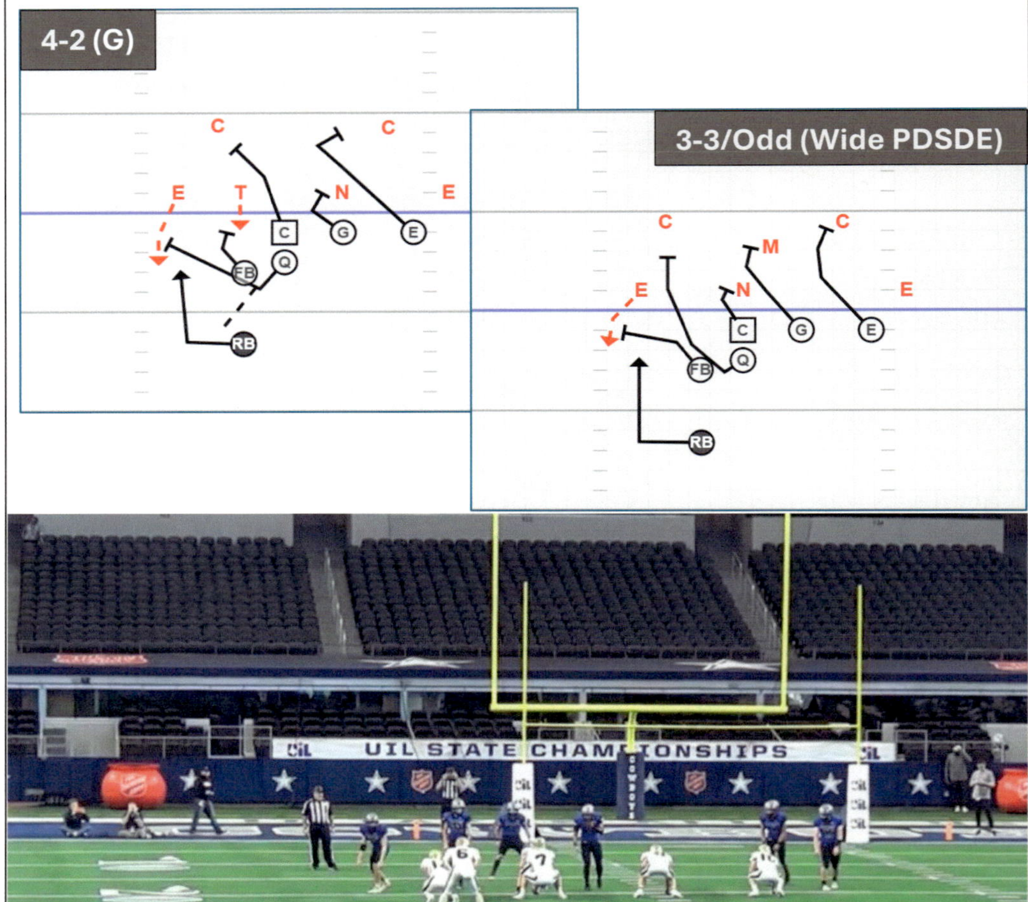


A Look at Abbott's Line Splits

What's a T.B.O?

| Set: | J-Bird | Team: | Benjamin |
|---|---|---|---|
| Play: | 3-Pass | Scheme: | T.B.O |

**Coaches Corner**

T.B.O stands for "Tailback Option." 6-man football hardly has any "true" R.P.O's. This is what we consider a "R.P.O" in our world.

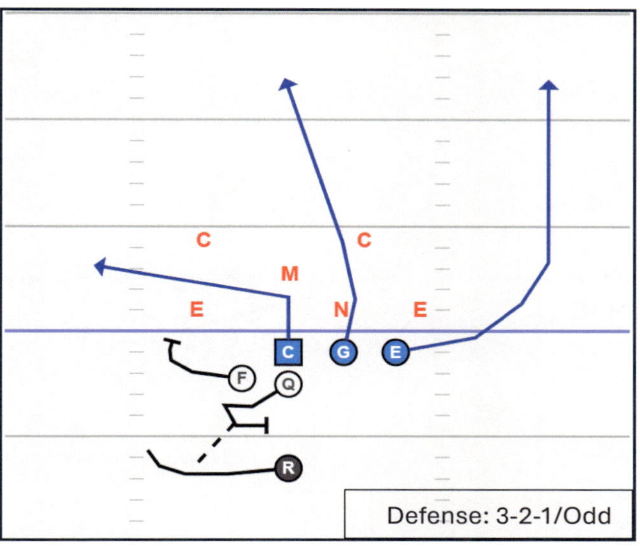


| C: | 3 Step "Slant-Flat" | QB: | Pitch wide – Peal Backside |
|---|---|---|---|
| G: | M.O.R – Pipe/Bend Route | FB: | Hook/Seal First man on Edge of LOS |
| TE: | Wide Vertical | RB: | Progression: Left to Right |

*The Clipboard*

Think of this as the greatest complaint to any sweep series you have in your offense. What's funny is that in the 6-man world, teams like Benjamin actually base around T.B.O's and instead use the run game to complaint it. If you have a special athlete who can run and throw well – T.B.O's would be a great install for you.

## Six-Man's "GT Counter"

**Coaches Corner**

If you were to use basic "G.O.D" rules. What's the difference on a **"Back" block?** It's when the Center can block a defender "Head up" backside.

| Set: | Wing | Team: | Whiteface |
|---|---|---|---|
| Play: | Wrap "Counter" | Scheme: | Gap |

Defense: 4-2 (Strong)

| C: | Back Block | QB: | Stay down midline for handoff |
|---|---|---|---|
| PSTE: | Down | FB: | Pull & wrap through for 2nd level |
| BSTE: | Pull & Kickout PSDE | RB: | One "Set Step" – Aim A gap to B gap. |

*The Clipboard*

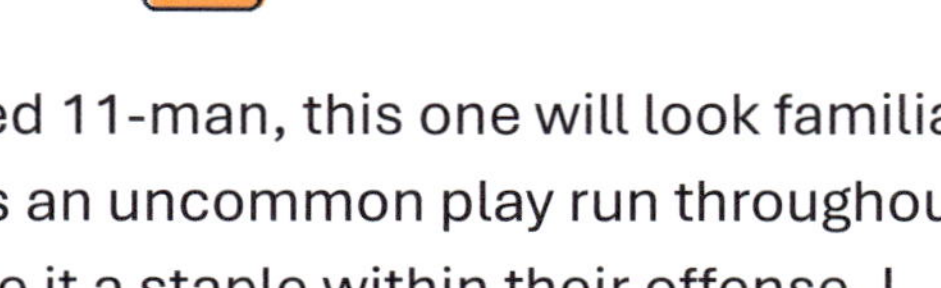

For anyone who's coached 11-man, this one will look familiar to you! Believe or not, this is an uncommon play run throughout 6-man. But Whiteface made it a staple within their offense. I consider this another version of the "Get downhill now" run game! The FB now "wrap" pulls and looks inside-out for his 2nd level defender to block.

## Single Route Play Action's

| Set: | J-Bird | Team: | Garden City |
|---|---|---|---|
| Play: | Corner - Iso | Scheme: | Play Action |

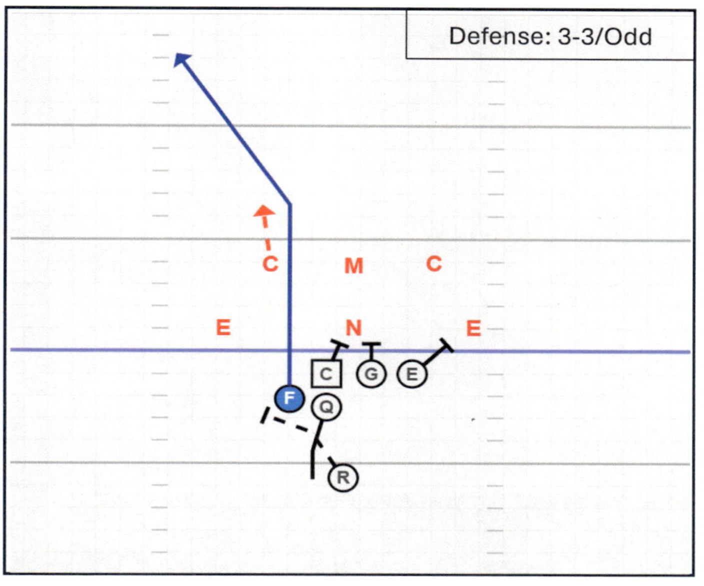


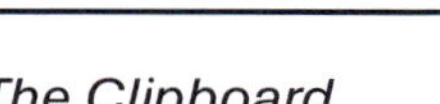

**Coaches Corner**

Garden City's J-Bird is different than most. They use tighter splits and put the RB strongside instead of weak.

| C: | Full Slide – A Gap | QB: | Hide ball in gut – Stay on midline |
|---|---|---|---|
| G: | B Gap to Help on A | FB: | Corner Route: Inside & Vertical – Break at 8-10 yards. |
| TE: | Full side - Edge | RB: | "Token" fake in Weak A gap |

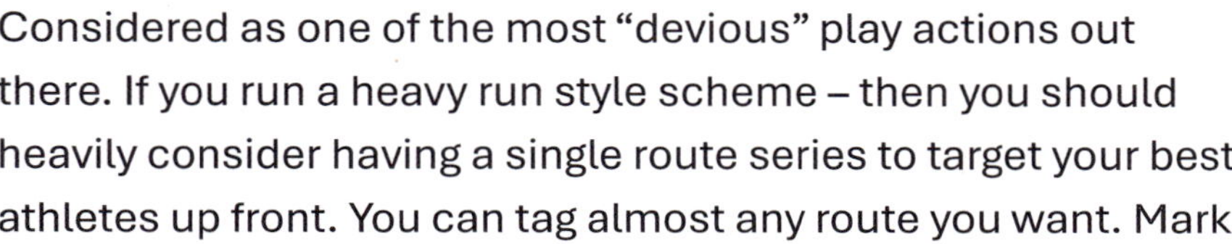

*The Clipboard*

Considered as one of the most "devious" play actions out there. If you run a heavy run style scheme – then you should heavily consider having a single route series to target your best athletes up front. You can tag almost any route you want. Mark this down as your "shot" play on your call sheet!

## More Variations

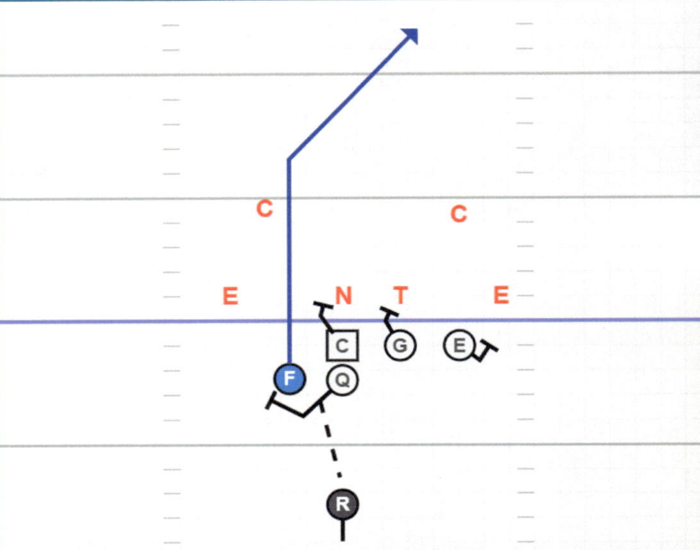


Newcastle will run Single Route T.B.O'S out of their Tight Sets.

Newcastle vs. Spur in the 1A-D2 Bi-District Playoffs; *Texas 1A Fan; 2024*

# Let's Go for a Dive

| Set: | T | Team: | Iredell |
|---|---|---|---|
| Play: | Quick Dive | Scheme: | Gap/Zone |

**Coaches Corner**

One of the great things about a successful Dive play – Is that the sweep fake itself should "block" 1-2 defenders without having to touch them!

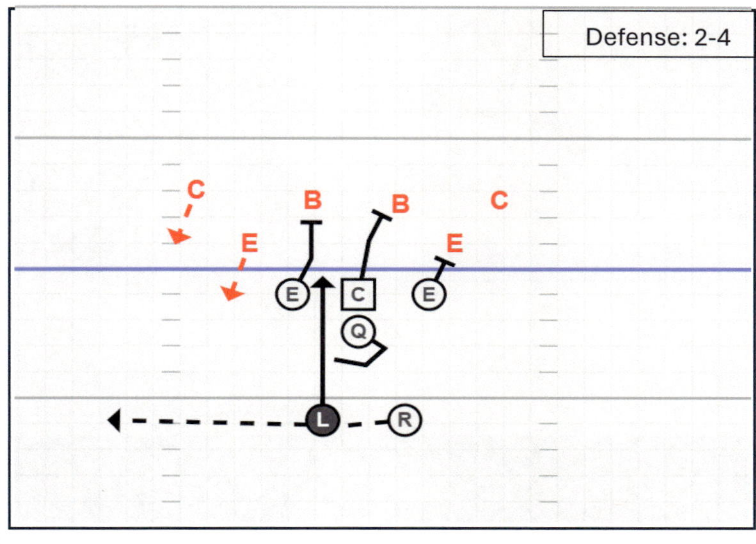


| C: | 2nd Level | QB: | Rotate out - Ball in HB's Belly. |
|---|---|---|---|
| PSTE: | 2nd Level | LHB: | Aim at A gap, Bend or Bounce |
| BSTE: | Back Block | RHB: | Stay Flat and sell Sweep |

*The Clipboard*

A play that can fit almost any tight set out there, Quick Dive is another complaint to the Sweep Series. Out of "T", this play gets quick downhill momentum and is great to give to your "Bruiser" backs. It can be considered a "zone" style play if you don't have any typical "down" blocks.

# More Variations

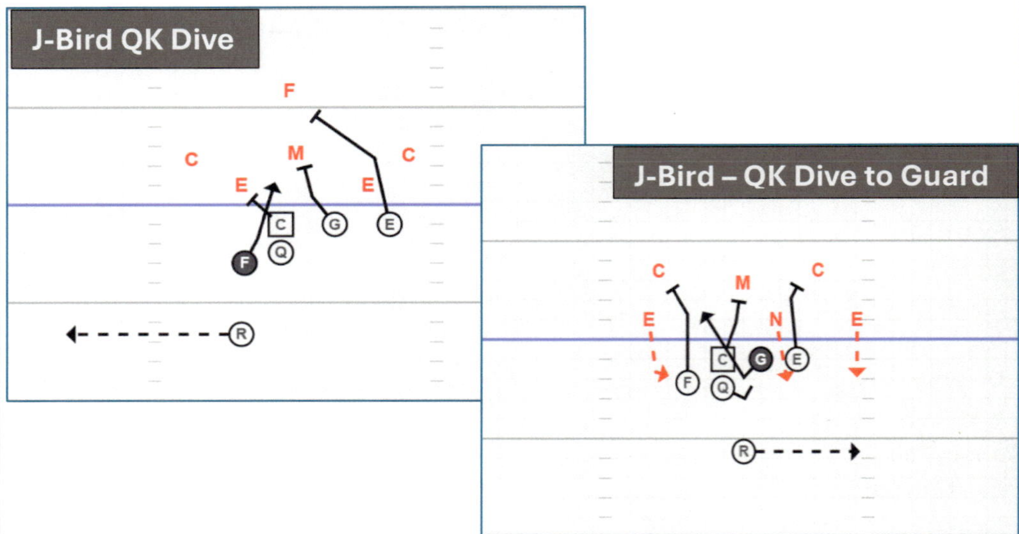


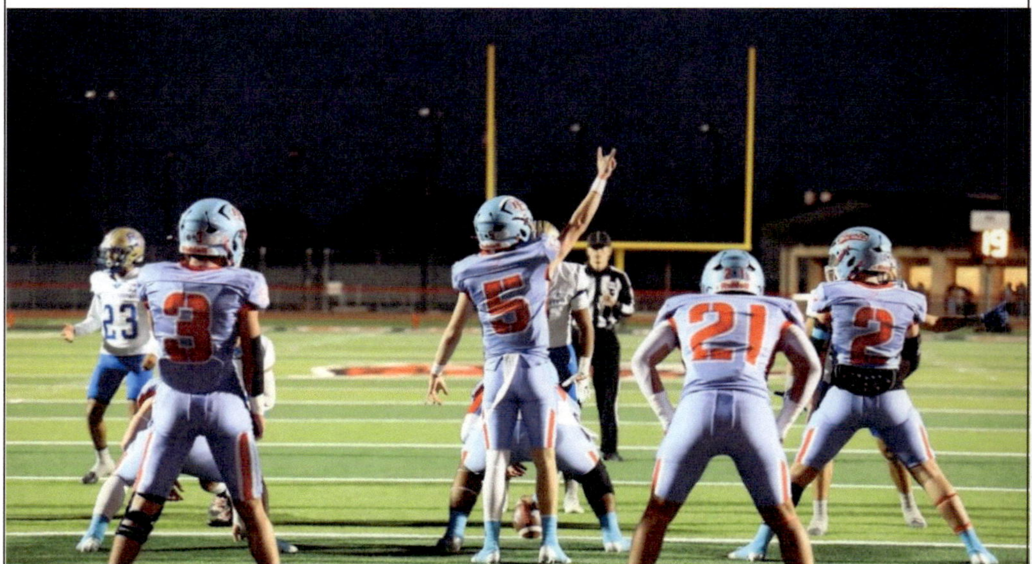


Borden County's "T" set vs. Buena Vista; *Texas 1A Fan; 2024*

The Ira "I"

**Coaches Corner**

Ira likes the FB real close! They will have him align with his hand at almost 2 yards!

| Set: | Eye | Team: | Ira |
|---|---|---|---|
| Play: | Sweep | Scheme: | Gap |

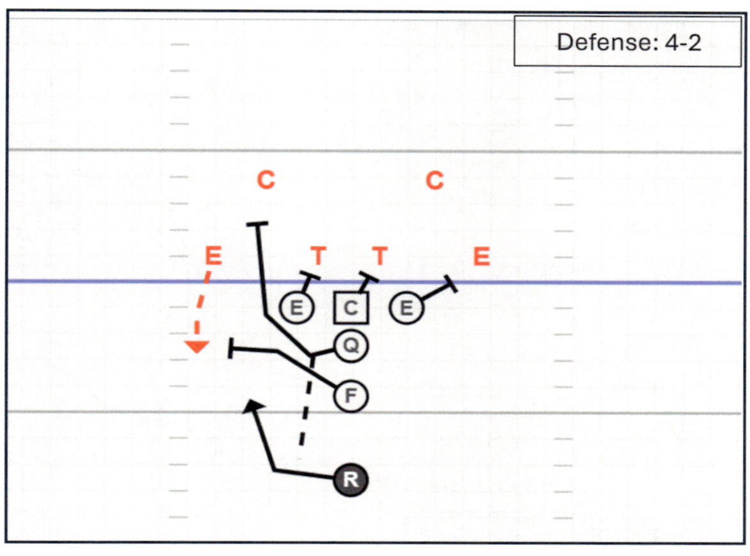


| C: | Down/Back | QB: | Open & Pitch – Lead to 2nd level |
|---|---|---|---|
| PSTE: | Down | FB: | Kickout or "Hook/Seal" PSDE |
| BSTE: | Down | RB: | 1 Sidestep – Get downhill now! |

*The Clipboard*

This looks familiar, doesn't it? Well of course! It's good old sweep once again. But I would kick myself If I didn't include the "Ira I." Ira may be one of the few teams in 6-man I've seen run the "I' practically full-time. They have been doing this for over nearly a decade and have had great success with it!

# Uno Reverse Card

| Set: | J-Bird | Team: | Klondike |
|---|---|---|---|
| Play: | Reverse | Scheme: | Gap |

## Coaches Corner

There are teams who will also run a version of Sweep to their TE. So you can also flip this reverse! (TE-FB)

Defense: 3-3 Strong

F

C C

E N E

E G C

Q F

R

1st Handoff – QB to FB

2nd Handoff – FB to TE

| C: | 2nd Level | QB: | Handoff to FB – Seal PSDE |
|---|---|---|---|
| G: | "On"/Seal/Hook | FB: | Handoff from behind QB – Handoff to TE with Back Hand. |
| TE: | Jab Step – Take handoff from FB | RB: | 2nd Level Edge |

*The Clipboard*

Everyone needs a GOTCHA play! One of my favorite misdirection plays in 6-man, this play is a perfect complaint to what many J-Bird teams call their "FB Sweep." (Essentially just another version of Sweep, but with a handoff). Another way to help make blocking easy on your athletes, when called at the right time. Defenders will help create "Setup" blocks to the playside.

My favorite dressing...Window Dressing!

**Coaches Corner**

**Motion** = Why not use it more? There is nearly a 70 % drop of motion used in 11-man compared to 6-man. Even with less guys, let's get moving more!

| **Set:** | J-Bird (Motion) | **Team:** | Happy |
|---|---|---|---|
| **Play:** | Corner/Flat | **Scheme:** | Play Action |

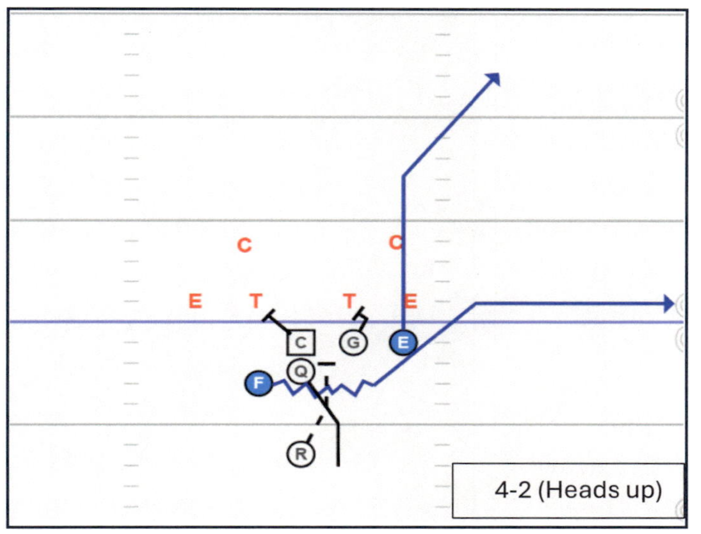


| **C:** | Back Block | **QB:** | Progression: Flat - Corner |
|---|---|---|---|
| **G:** | Seal/Hook | **FB:** | Motion over – Flat no deeper then 2-3 yards |
| **TE:** | 8-10 Yard Corner | **RB:** | Sell Fake – Protect A Gap |

*The Clipboard*

Generally, a great Tight Play Action Staple, a "Flood" concept can define as any 2-man High-Low combo to one side of the field. Happy shows a great example of how to "Window dress" a common play already in your offense. The great part is, is that this motion can turn into a great 3-4 play series for you!

## Use your backs in the Pass Game!

### *Coaches Corner*

**Pro**: This is an awesome P.A against Odd fronts since you are attacking the middle of the field. **Con:** Pass protection here is not great against a heavy front

| **Set:** | T | **Team:** | Rankin |
|---|---|---|---|
| **Play:** | Post/Seam | **Scheme:** | Play Action |

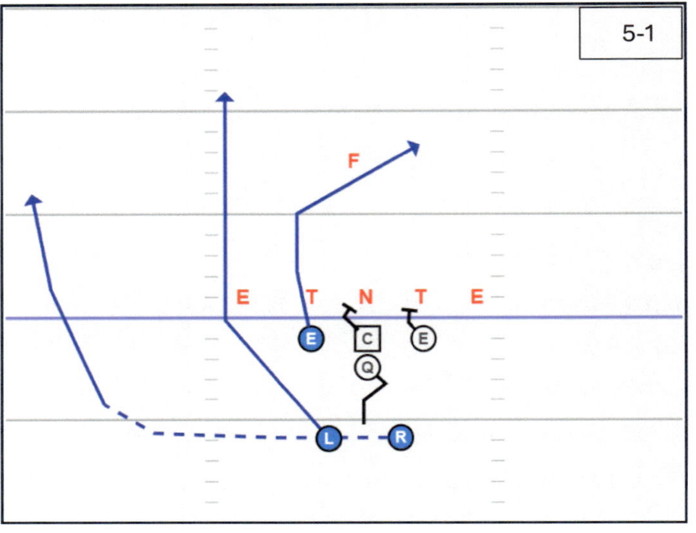


| **C:** | Hook/Seal | **QB:** | Progression: Post – Seam - Wheel |
|---|---|---|---|
| **PSTE:** | Quick 5 Yard Post | **LHB:** | Vertical Seam (Inside Hash) |
| **BSTE:** | Hook/Seal | **RHB:** | Sell Sweep – Slow Up field Wheel |

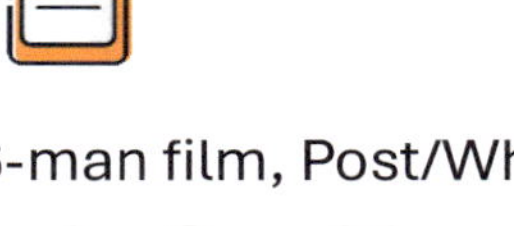

*The Clipboard*

If you were to dive deeper in 6-man film, Post/Wheel Play actions is a popular 2-man combo. One of the reasons it's so loved is that the Post can clear out a lot of 1-high and even 2-high looks. In Sets like the "T" the back who ends up on the "Seam/Wheel" tends to be forgotten about.

## 6-Man's Tush Push?

| **Set:** | Turtle | **Team:** | Christian School at Castle Hills |
|---|---|---|---|
| **Play:** | QK Dive | **Scheme:** | Short Yardage |

*Coaches Corner*

Invented by Fredericksburg – Heritage, the Turtle set uses foot to foot splits and usually puts their biggest kid like a FB or Guard in the backfield!

Defense: 3-3 Strong

| **C:** | Back Block | **QB:** | Handoff to FB |
|---|---|---|---|
| **G:** | Down | **FB:** | Aim off TE's outside hip |
| **TE:** | Down | **RB:** | Kickout Edge/PSDE |

*The Clipboard*

If you have watched any football on Sunday's recently, you've most likely seen what's known as the "Tush Push." But with the QB sneak being non-existent in 6-man, I personally believe that this is "Six Man's Tush Push." It is one of the best short yardage sets I've ever seen. I personally had to coach against it last season...TWICE! It nearly seemed like this set almost always converted a first down.

# Student Body Right

| Set: | Heavy | Team: | Cherokee |
|---|---|---|---|
| Play: | Sweep | Scheme: | Gap/Zone |

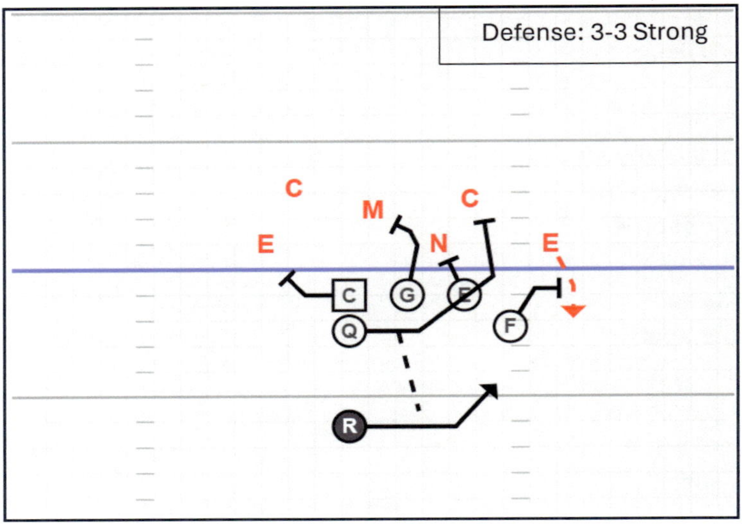

## *Coaches Corner*

In the 1960's USC popularized a play called "Study Body Right." And it's as simple as it sounds! They would pull everyone they could and GO!

Defense: 3-3 Strong

| C: | Back Block | QB: | Pitch to RB – 2nd Level |
|---|---|---|---|
| G: | 2nd Level | FB: | Kickout/Seal PSDE |
| TE: | Down | RB: | Get Flat – Read FB's Block |

### *The Clipboard*

Why not line up everyone on one side of the ball and get after it! Although this is not their base set, in the clip attached Cherokee seems to use this as a "pace play." They seem to line up in this set as quick as possible to give the defense almost zero time to adjust pre-snap. A great idea to add to your offense as an extra tweak!

# Your QB is an Athlete too!

**Coaches Corner**

With the exchange rule in 6-man, it can be tricky finding ways to get your QB involved in your offense. Using him as a receiving threat is one way to do that!

| **Set:** | J-Bird | **Team:** | Jayton |
|---|---|---|---|
| **Play:** | QB Wheel | **Scheme:** | Play Action/Gadget |

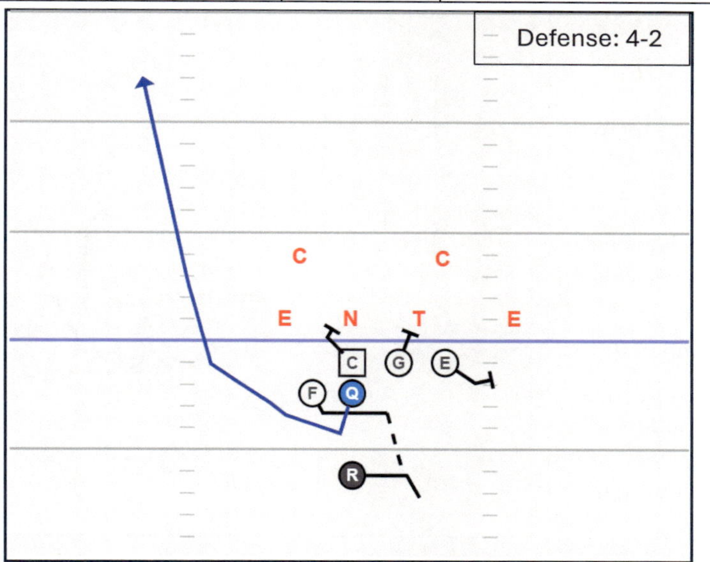


| **C:** | On (Hook/Seal) | **QB:** | Handoff to FB – Get Vertical and wide |
|---|---|---|---|
| **G:** | Down | **FB:** | Get handoff – Pitch to RB – Protect A Gap to BSDE |
| **TE:** | Down/Pass Pro Slide | **RB:** | Take Pitch – Throw to QB |

*The Clipboard*

Find ways to make any play you run look the same! Jayton sells a FB Sweep (Or even a speed option) very well here and keeps all the blocking rules the same up front! All that changes is the QB tagged on a wheel route. Find the simplest ways to make small tweaks to things you already run! “Few plays, many ways!”

## Best Tool in the Toolbox?

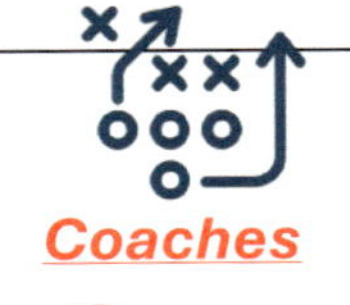

**Coaches Corner**

Straight off the Abbott Coaching Tree, Blum has had lots of success with their version of the J-Bird. Including a State Championship in 2019.

| **Set:** | J-Bird (Split) | **Team:** | Blum |
|---|---|---|---|
| **Play:** | Hammer | **Scheme:** | Gap |

Defense: 3-3/Odd

| **C:** | On (Seal/Hook) | **QB:** | Blind "Flip" Pitch – Get to 2nd Level |
|---|---|---|---|
| **G:** | 2nd Level | **FB:** | Pull Across – Kickout PSDE |
| **TE:** | "Decoy" Fade | **RB:** | 1 Sidestep – Get Downhill |

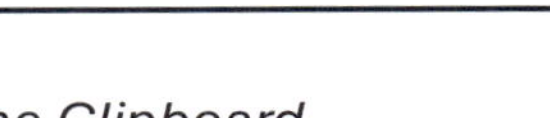

*The Clipboard*

Another 6-man Staple, "Hammer" is a version of strong sweep where the FB pulls across as the Kickout man (Some teams prefer the QB as the kickout). Like in the example above, lots of J-Bird systems like the ability to split their TE out wide and still be able to run their base handful of plays. Splitting out a WR opposite, can help space things out and make run fits challenging for 2nd level defenders.

# More Variations

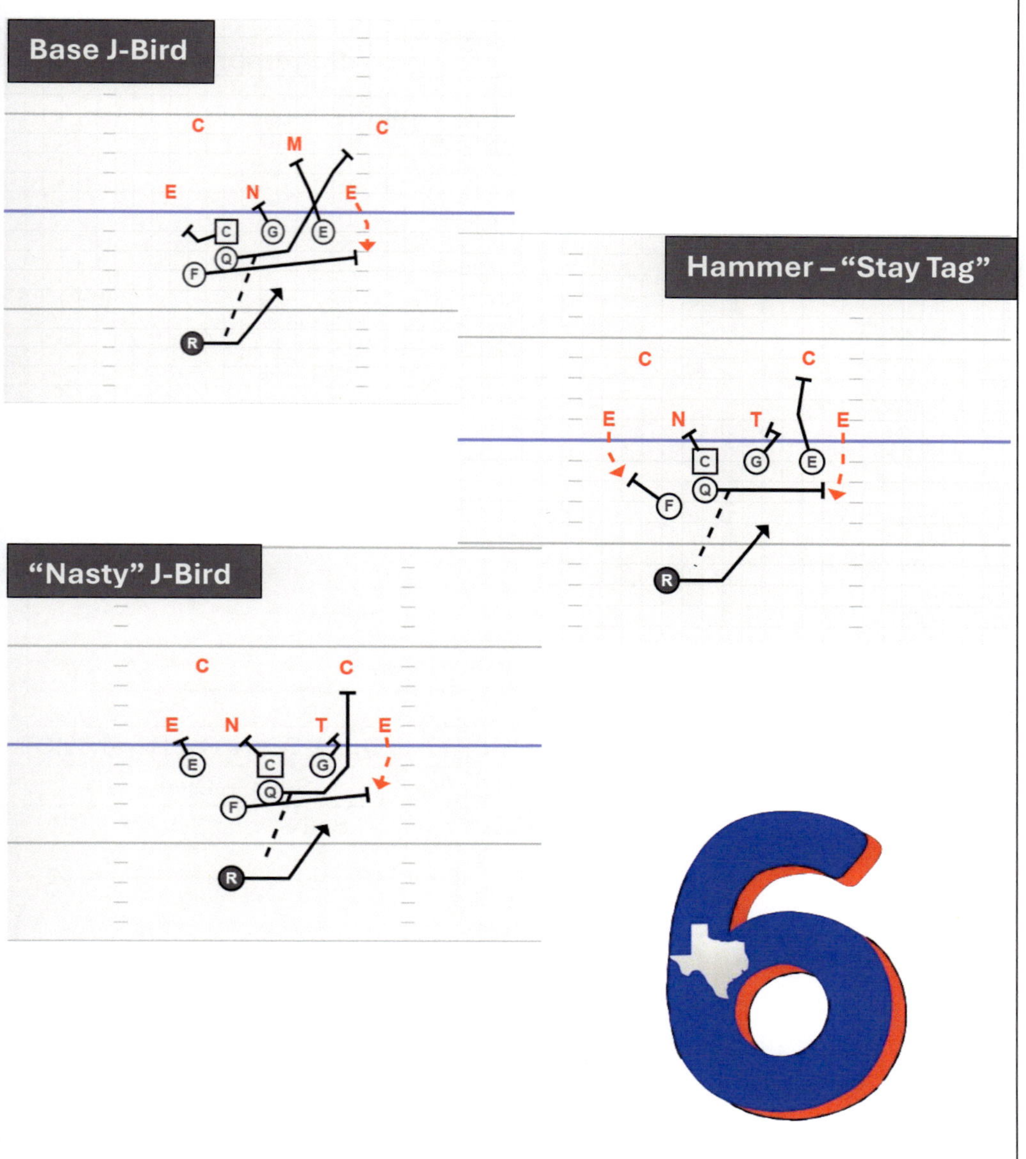

## Sneaky, Sneaky!

| Set: | J-Bird | Team: | May |
|---|---|---|---|
| Play: | Fake Dive – Sneak Pass | Scheme: | Play Action |

**Coaches Corner**

I would argue that 6-man schemes allow you to be even more creative then 11-man. Don't always try and fit a square peg into a round hole. Take 10 minutes to draw your base plays with 1 creative tag to it!

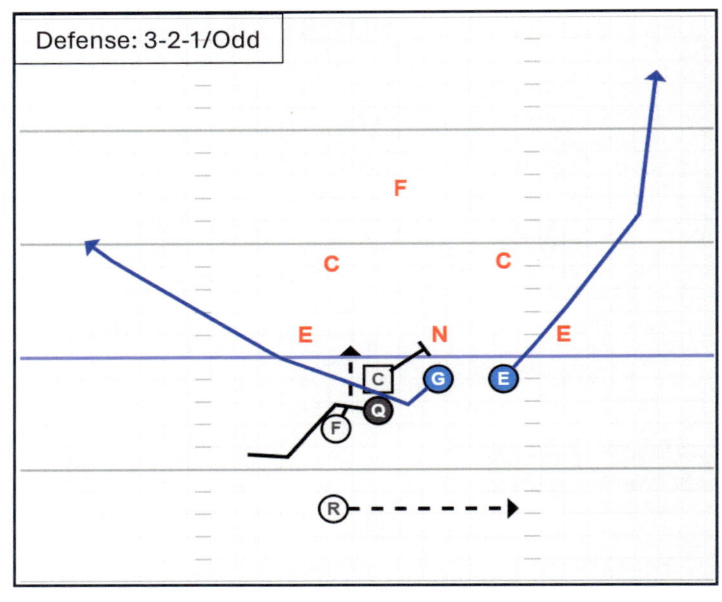


| C: | Back Block | QB: | Fake Quick Dive – Get Depth **FAST** |
|---|---|---|---|
| G: | Trap pull – Slip behind PSDE | FB: | Sell QK Dive |
| TE: | Wide Vertical | RB: | Sell Strong Sweep |

*The Clipboard*

One of my favorite things to see from Tight teams, is finding ways to pair a Play action with any run they carry. You rarely see Play Action off a Fake Quick Dive yet May has a creative way of doing it! The Guard "tucking" under the dive on a trap pull is genius here, as it puts the Corner's eyes on the dive instead of the Guard who is sneaking into the flat.

Every good Attack needs a COUNTERattack

## Coaches Corner

Cutback counter can fit into just about any set out there. A main component needed in this scheme; Playside TE or FB to protect the A Gap.

| **Set:** | T | **Team:** | Buena Vista |
|---|---|---|---|
| **Play:** | Cutback Counter | **Scheme:** | Gap |

Defense: 2-2-2 (Head up)

| **C:** | Back Block | **QB:** | Open like it's sweep – Once Back has ball – Plant and get to 2nd level |
|---|---|---|---|
| **PSTE:** | On (Hook/Seal) | **LHB:** | Open to sweep – Get Ball – Plant & read Trap Block |
| **BSTE:** | Trap Pull – Kickout PSDE/Edge | **RHB:** | Sweep Rules – Kickout PSDE/EDGE |

*The Clipboard*

The purest form of a "Gap scheme" out there! Think of cutback counter as just another version of sweep = two lead blockers with a kickout. Counter does the same action! The goal here is, that we take the LB's and get them moving in the wrong direction, giving our blocks more time to setup.

# More Variations

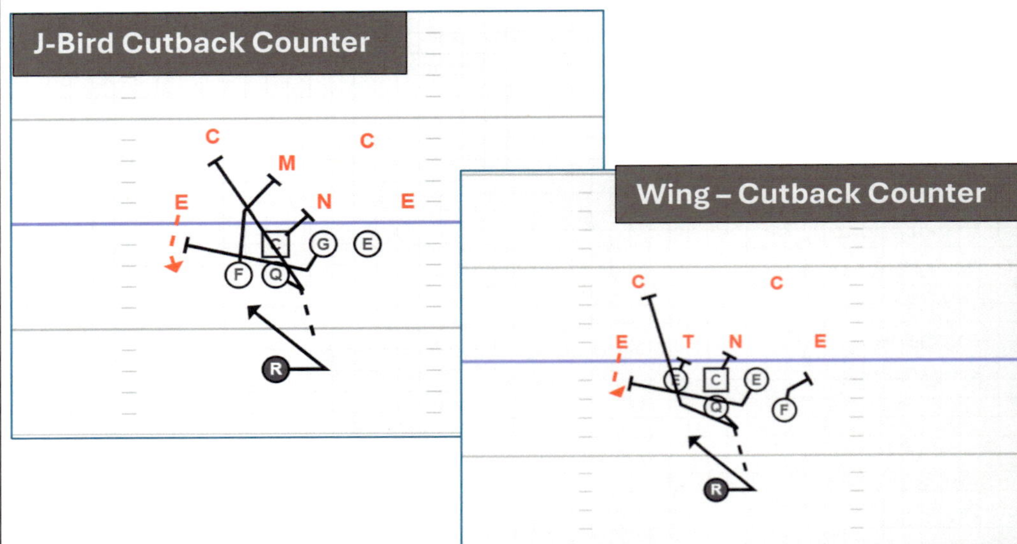

Buena Vista in "Wing" vs. Union Hill; *Texas 1A Fan; 2024*

Army, Navy, and Air Force!

| Set: | J-bird (Split) | Team: | Balmorhea |
|---|---|---|---|
| Play: | Speed Option | Scheme: | Gap |

Defense: 4-2

**Coaches Corner**

A popular scheme used by the academies for having smaller athletes. Option football has been used as a staple at places like Balmorhea & Garden City.

| C: | Down | QB: | Handoff (Behind) Block BSDE |
|---|---|---|---|
| G: | Down | FB: | Take handoff – Read PSDE as pitchman |
| TE: | (WR) Stalk block | RB: | Open Step – 4 x 4 yd. Spacing |

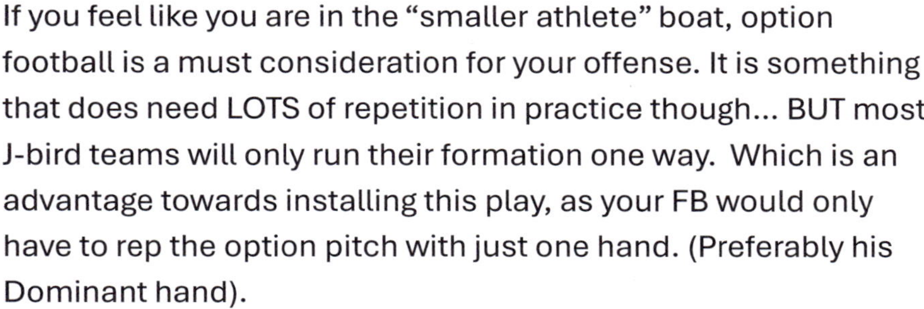

*The Clipboard*

If you feel like you are in the "smaller athlete" boat, option football is a must consideration for your offense. It is something that does need LOTS of repetition in practice though… BUT most J-bird teams will only run their formation one way. Which is an advantage towards installing this play, as your FB would only have to rep the option pitch with just one hand. (Preferably his Dominant hand).

3…2…1…

**Coaches Corner**

**Zone Block teaching points** = Playside foot wide & lateral, front hand in playside armpit, back hand should end up center of breastplate.

| **Set:** | T | **Team:** | Jonesboro |
|---|---|---|---|
| **Play:** | FK Sweep - Rocket | **Scheme:** | Zone |

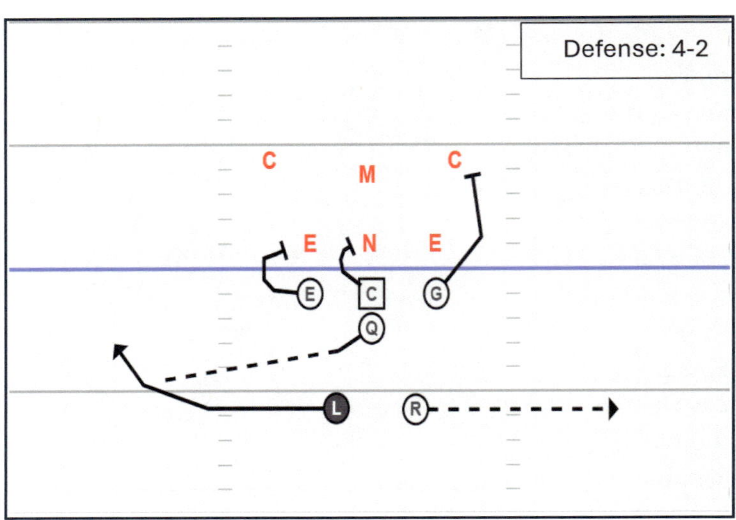


| **C:** | On (Hook/Seal) | **QB:** | Rocket Pitch to LHB |
|---|---|---|---|
| **PSTE:** | On (Hook/Seal) | **LHB:** | FAST Sweep path – Get to Sideline |
| **BSTE:** | False Pull | **RHB:** | Fast Sell Sweep |

*The Clipboard*

Not a "Flashy" play by any means, but one would be surprised the simplicity of "Eye candy" and how by only just having to pull 2 players giving the presentation of sweep – while running a "Rocket sweep" opposite. To be able to do this successfully, we do have to "Zone" reach the defense. This is also a play that should be called against the correct defensive front.

Your Center is a hidden talent!

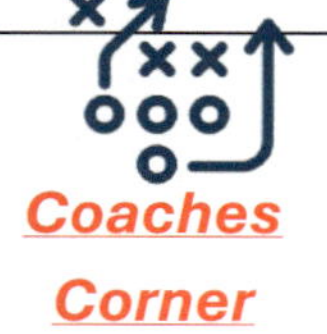

**Coaches Corner**

If you ever hear a call from a defense saying "Dead!" This is referring to the QB having no exchanges given to him, meaning that his is ineligible to run and therefore "Dead."

| **Set:** | T | **Team:** | Strawn |
|---|---|---|---|
| **Play:** | Drop Back | **Scheme:** | 3-Step DBP |

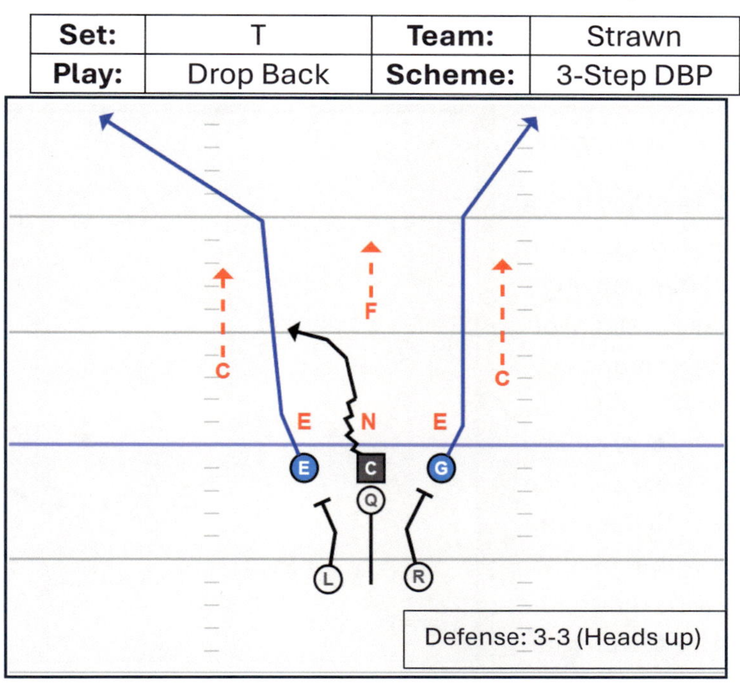


| **C:** | 3 Count Block – Release into Flat | **QB:** | Progression: Corners - Center |
|---|---|---|---|
| **LTE:** | 10 Yard Corner | **LHB:** | Protect – A Gap to B Gap |
| **RTE:** | 10 Yard Corner | **RHB:** | Protect – A Gap to B Gap |

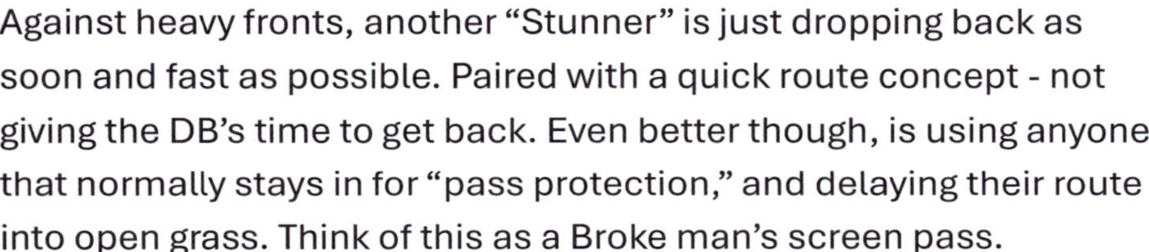

*The Clipboard*

Against heavy fronts, another "Stunner" is just dropping back as soon and fast as possible. Paired with a quick route concept - not giving the DB's time to get back. Even better though, is using anyone that normally stays in for "pass protection," and delaying their route into open grass. Think of this as a Broke man's screen pass.

*Three of a Kind*

| **Set:** | J-Bird (Motion) | **Team:** | Three-Way |
|---|---|---|---|
| **Play:** | Post/Wheel | **Scheme:** | Sweep Pass |

**Coaches Corner**

Three-Way had a historic season in 2024, making their first playoff appearance in school history. They also racked up 9 wins, which is also the same number of total wins they had since the program launched in 2018.

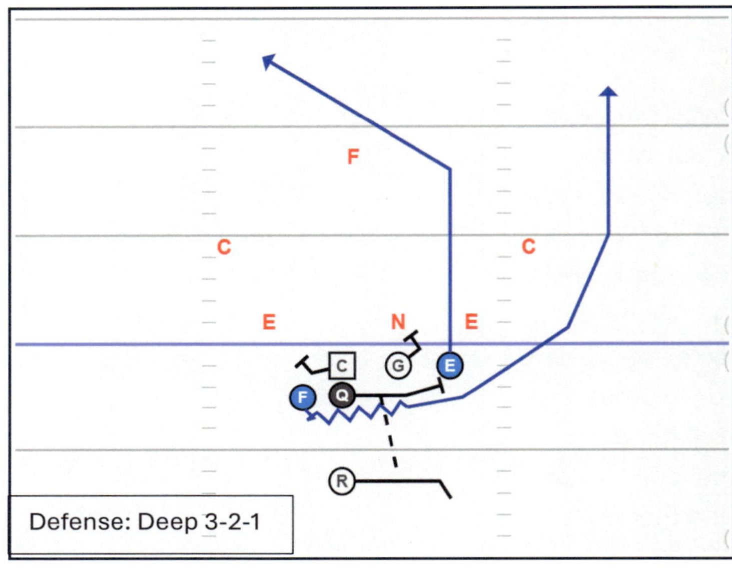


| **C:** | Back Block | **QB:** | Sweep Pitch – kickout PSDE |
|---|---|---|---|
| **G:** | On (Hook/Seal) | **FB:** | Motion - Wheel |
| **TE:** | 8-10 Yard Post | **RB:** | Progression: Post - Wheel |

*The Clipboard*

A preference some teams have when running strong sweep is to use a “Motion series” to get to it, instead of pulling the FB across (Hammer). So, if this something you like doing in your offense, you need answers to when the defense see’s this pre-snap and thinks “Oh man, here’s strong sweep again.” Once again, to nail this home – Disguise your complaint plays layered with your “hang your hat” plays!

# More Variations

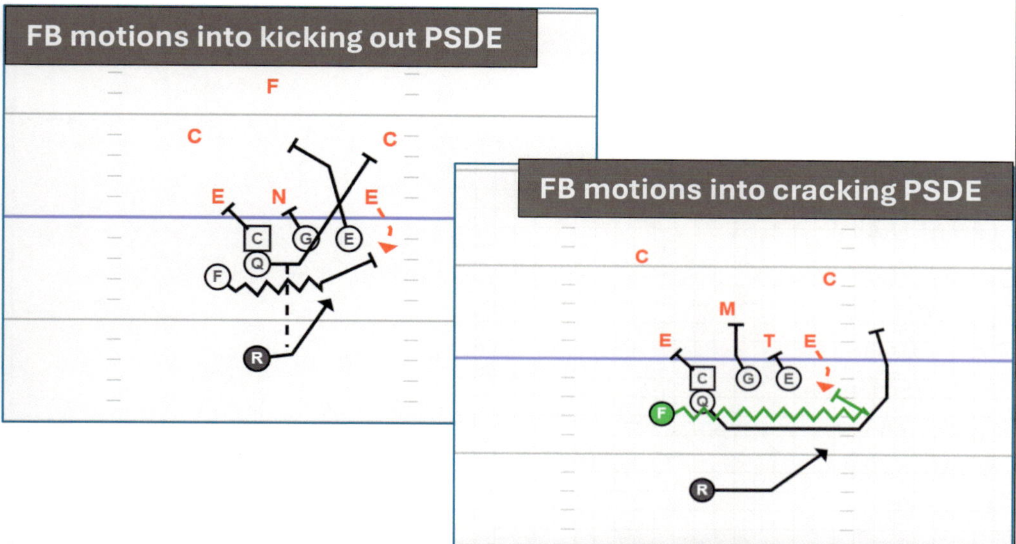

Three Way in "J-Bird" vs. Iredell; *Texas 1A Fan; 2024*

| Set: | J-bird (Split) | Team: | Union Hill |
|---|---|---|---|
| Play: | Iso WR - Post | Scheme: | T.B.O |

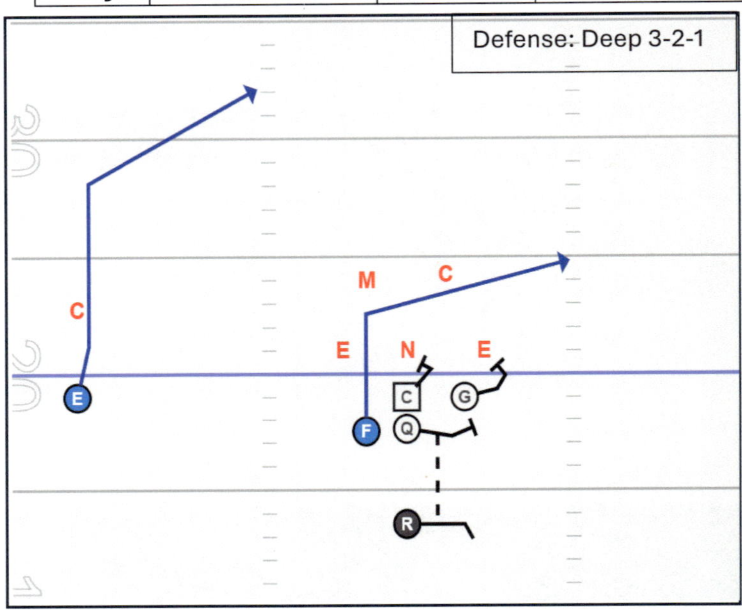


## Coaches Corner

**Did you know?**

Out of 154 teams in UIL 1A, only **10** are East of the Dallas-Fort Worth area. Union hill is one of those teams, about 45 minutes outside of Tyler, Texas.

| C: | On (Hook/Seal) | QB: | Pitch – Pass Pro on Edge |
|---|---|---|---|
| G: | On (Hook/Seal) | FB: | 3 Step Slant |
| TE: | 10-12 Yard Post | RB: | Progression: Post - Slant |

*The Clipboard*

Although it's a rarity in 6-man to have the opportunity to just drop back and throw Isolated 50/50 balls to stud WR's. That doesn't mean that sometimes our 2nd or maybe even best athlete is at TE! Splitting him out in a common set you may already run and just adding to your "T.B.O" series, also gives one of your better athletes at RB the chance to run if your "Iso" route isn't there!

...Takeoff

| Set: | J-Bird | Team: | Water Valley |
|---|---|---|---|
| Play: | Fake Quick Dive - Rocket | Scheme: | Gap |

**Coaches Corner**

If you ever want to consider installing a "Rocket" play. Remember the PSDE is unblocked = Therefore you need to find a way to Freeze him!

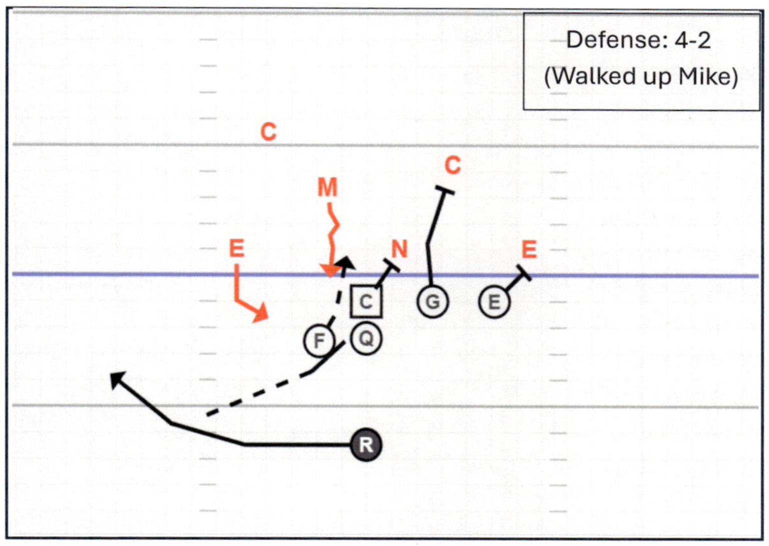


| C: | Down | QB: | Token Fake to FB – Rocket pitch out to RB |
|---|---|---|---|
| G: | 2nd Level | FB: | Sell QK Dive – Pick up A Gap |
| TE: | Back Block | RB: | Fly to edge – Rocket Sweep |

*The Clipboard*

The compliment play to the compliment play! While Quick Dive is your best Inside/Misdirection hitting play in the J-bird set it can also be the easiest to "Stuff" with enough downhill momentum by any Linebacker. Water Valley times up a great play here to counter the aggressive A Gap penetration.

The Pasadena Wing

| Set: | Wing | Team: | Pasadena First Baptist |
|---|---|---|---|
| Play: | Waggle | Scheme: | Play Action |

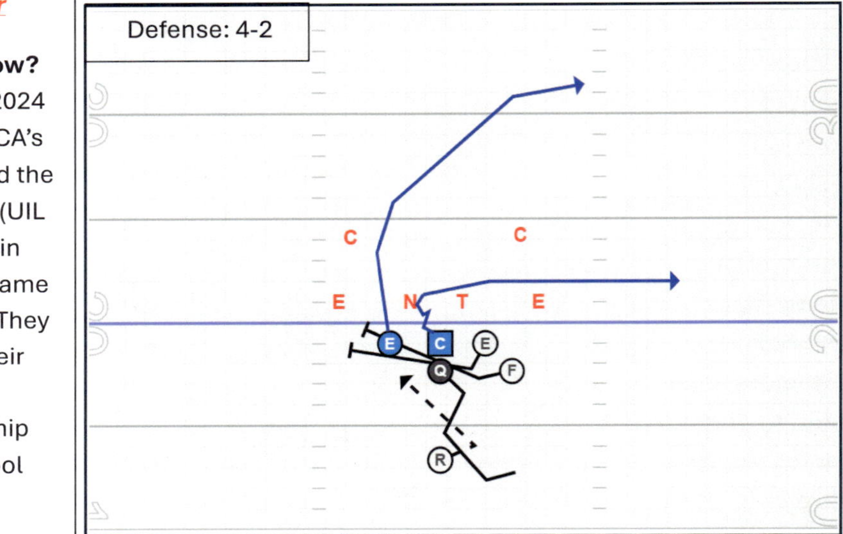


**Coaches Corner**

**Did you know?** That in the 2024 Season, FBCA's Offense lead the entire state (UIL and TAPPS) in points per game with 69.15. They also won their first State championship ever in school history.

| C: | Chip – Get Flat | QB: | Progression: Center - TE |
|---|---|---|---|
| BSTE: | 10-12 Yard Cross | FB: | Pull up & in like it's "Wrap" |
| PSTE: | Pull like it's "Wrap" | RB: | Jab step – Sell Fake |

*The Clipboard*

Talk about marrying two plays! If you missed it, go checkout Whiteface's "Wrap Counter" play (Page 38.) Everything looks the **EXACT** same here, all that is simply added on here is that we now release the Center & BSTE towards the way they were blocking anyways!

| Set: | J-Bird | Team: | Coolidge |
|---|---|---|---|
| Play: | Bootleg | Scheme: | Play Action |

**Coaches Corner**

(FB's Route) – Inside stem or outside steam? (The first 2 steps of his route). He inside stems here to grab the MLB **AND** PSCB's eyes down.

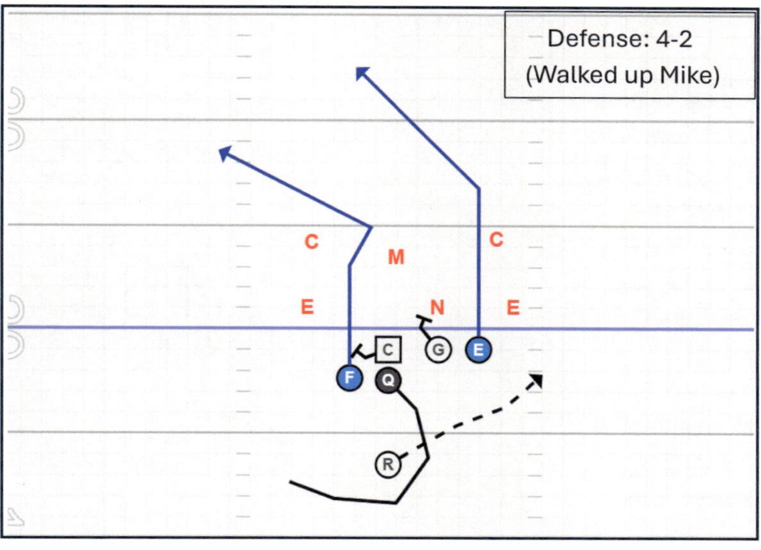


| C: | Pass pro - Edge | QB: | Progression: Post - Corner |
|---|---|---|---|
| G: | On (Hook/Seal) | FB: | Stick Post-Corner |
| TE: | 7-8 Yard Post | RB: | Sell Strong Sweep |

*The Clipboard*

Although the best play action can typically be a 1-2 punch high-low action. We see an interesting design here that is mainly meant to try and get a post open with no middle coverage help. The only hope left for the defense in this scenario is indeed the weakside Cornerback...who gets occupied by the corner route!

## Time to DRAW one in the Dirt

| Set: | J-Bird | Team: | Valley |
|---|---|---|---|
| Play: | Draw | Scheme: | Drop Back |

### *Coaches Corner*

A straight "Drop Back" from Tight sets can almost be seen as a part of the "Play Action Family." It is treated more as a "Stunner" to the defense then the traditional "5-step drop."

Defense: 3-3 (Tight)

| C: | On (Hook/Seal) | QB: | 3 Step Drop |
|---|---|---|---|
| G: | Down | FB: | 2nd Level |
| TE: | 2nd Level | RB: | Shuffle, Shuffle – Downhill! |

*The Clipboard*

An incredible call on 4th long, you'd think that a pass had to be coming...right? WRONG! Valley dials up an awesome design that complaints their drop back pass series. Draw in itself might be considered an "outdated scheme" in football, but it is the **BEST** possible complaint if you include your QB heavily in your pass game.

# The Glorified Fullback

| Set: | J-Bird | Team: | Houston Westbury |
|---|---|---|---|
| Play: | Counter Pass | Scheme: | Gap |

**Coaches Corner**

If there is any "Hidden Team" out there that you should study… it needs to be Westbury! Throughout 12 Games in 2024 they ran the ball 95 % of time only using 6-7 plays. Putting up a record of 9-3.

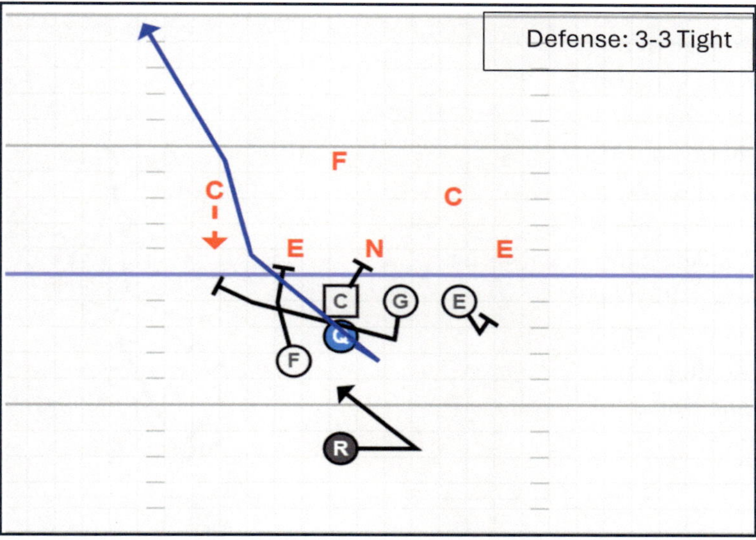


| C: | Down | QB: | Pitch – Slip through second level |
|---|---|---|---|
| G: | Pull – Kickout Edge | FB: | On (Hook/Seal) |
| TE: | Back Block | RB: | Counter Step – Pull up at LOS |

*The Clipboard*

With Westbury only passing 10 times all season, their QB did not have one pass attempt. Basically, Creating a two-fullback offense! Cutback counter was their favorite weakside play and one could see why! With the defense having eyes on the guard and seeing the pull action, the QB can slip right behind the defense into open grass!

| Set: | Unbalanced Eye | Team: | Sterling City |
|---|---|---|---|
| Play: | Sweep | Scheme: | Gap |

Coaches Corner

Although moving up to 11-man in 2022, Sterling City won the 1A-D1 state Title in 2020, finishing 15-0. And crazy enough their first ever year in 11-man they went 7-5 and won a playoff game!

Defense: 3-3 Strong (Head up)

C M C N T E C G E Q F R

| C: | On (Hook/Seal) | QB: | Rotate out; Pitch – 2nd Level |
|---|---|---|---|
| G: | On (Hook/Seal | FB: | Kickout PSDE |
| TE: | **“Down” Tag** = 2nd Level | RB: | Reset Step – Read FB’s block |

*The Clipboard*

**DOWN TAG =** We get a perfect example of a tag you should highly consider adding into your blocking scheme. You can call this however you like, but a “Down” tag refers to when I am covered as a Lineman – I can leave him for the 2nd level. Now if you recall, typically if you’re covered you want to execute a “On” block. But in this case, we will block that man with the FB!

# More Variations

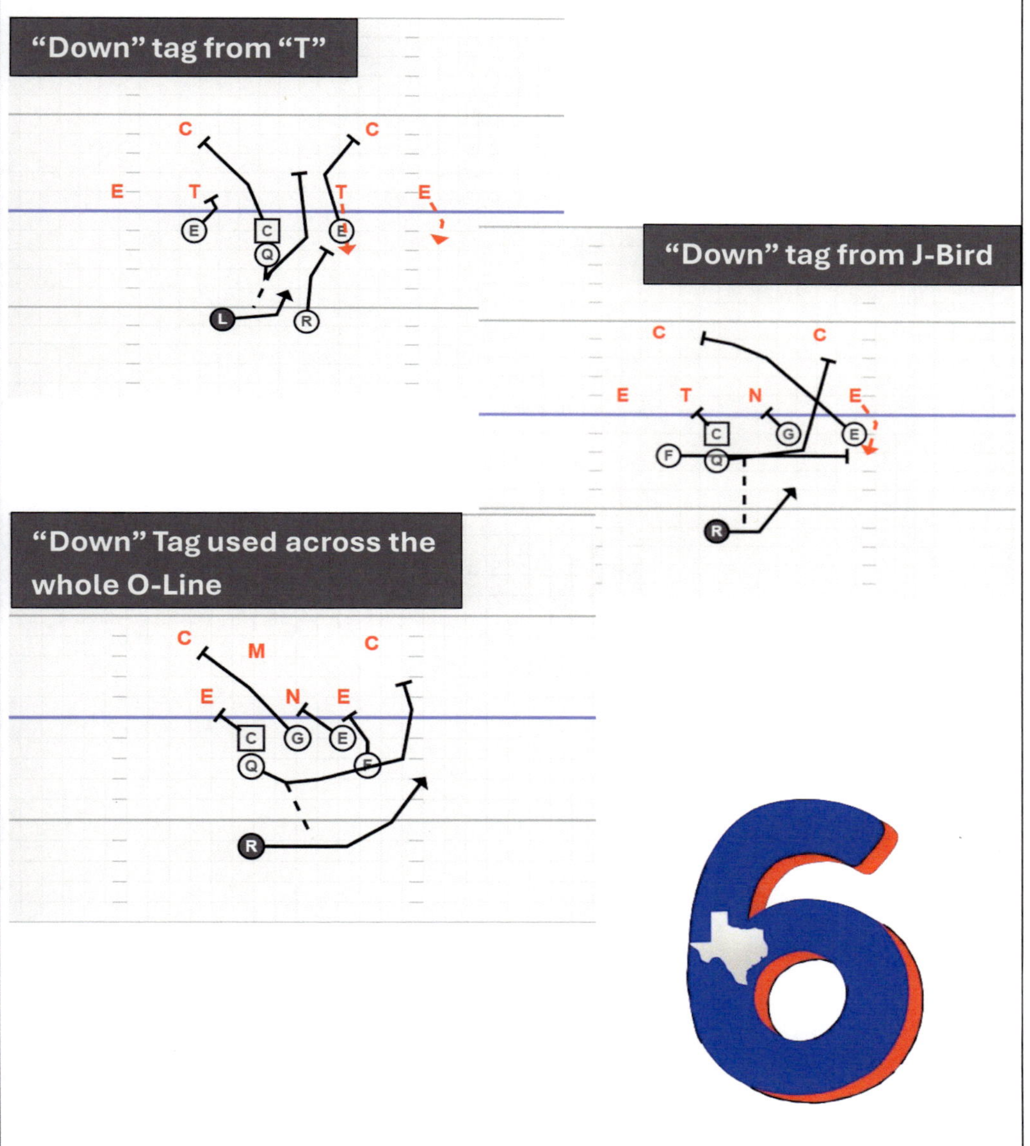

# Hybrid

The Name “Hybrid” came from the idea of a combination of both Tight & Spread sets. The same rules apply from Tight offenses, where we will never have more the 1 WR in the formation, BUT instead we are now backed up in the shotgun.

Typically, with Hybrid sets, the “End’s” have wider splits than most. Sometimes almost up to 5 yards wide.

It is common in a lot of Hybrid systems to see defenses line up almost every Defensive Lineman “Head up” on the End’s. This is done to counter the fact that the offense is mainly taking bigger splits to create a greater angle for a down block.

Knox City’s Wide splits with all 3 “linemen” being covered

Extra Page for Notes & Diagrams

Extra Page for Notes & Diagrams

Give that Dog a Bone!

| **Set:** | Bone | **Team:** | Knox City |
|---|---|---|---|
| **Play:** | Sweep | **Scheme:** | Gap/Zone |

***Coaches Corner***

Wide Splits = Natural running lanes. Knox City's WR's splits can vary from anywhere to 3-4 yards (9-12 Feet.)

Defense: 4-2 (Heads up)

| **C:** | 2nd Level | **QB:** | Open Pitch – 2nd Level |
|---|---|---|---|
| **PSWR:** | On (Hook/Seal) | **LHB:** | 1 Sidestep = Read PSHB's block |
| **BSWR:** | On (Hook/Seal) | **RHB:** | Kickout PSDE |

*The Clipboard*

I absolutely had to kickoff this section off with Knox City's bone. Splits can matter with anything you install, but "flexing" out a defense could be the simplest solution you didn't know you needed! Knox city has been a prime example that you absolutely can still run the rock with smaller athletes. They can create natural running lanes with wider angles!

# More Variations

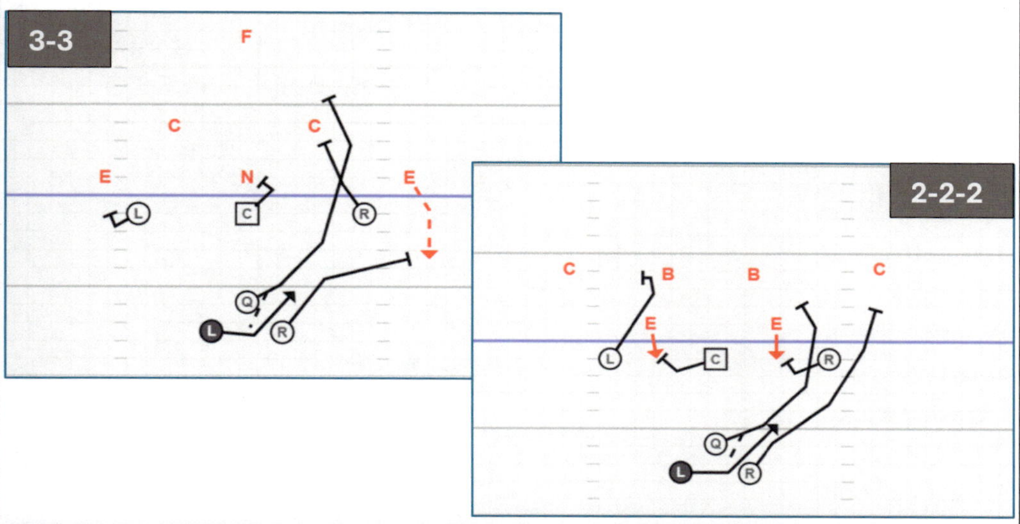

*Knox City running Sweep vs. Paducah; Texas 1A Fan; 2024*

We call it "Streetball"

| **Set:** | Bullet | **Team:** | Richland Springs |
|---|---|---|---|
| **Play:** | Post/Cross | **Scheme:** | T.B.O |

**Coaches Corner**

It's common in Spread/Hybrid to have a position that's referred to as "SpreadBack." Think of this player as your "Swiss Army Knife"

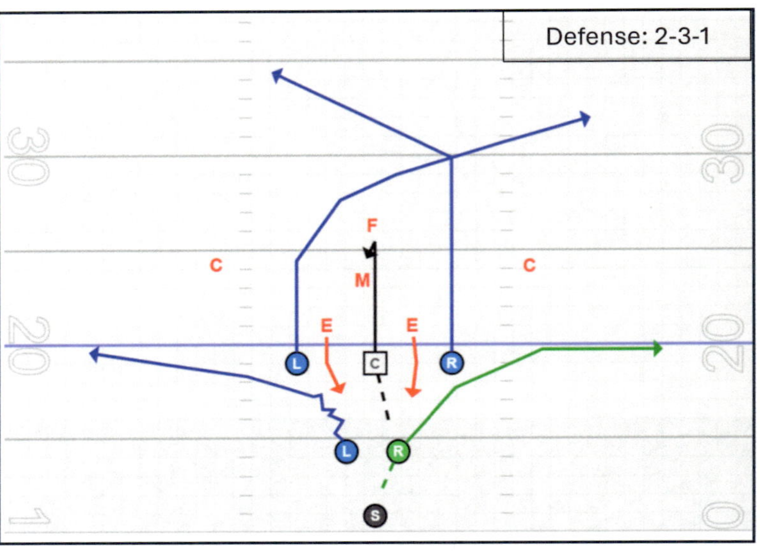


| **C:** | 5 Yard Curl | **SB:** | Progression: Cross – Flats - Center |
|---|---|---|---|
| **RWR:** | 10 Yard Post | **LUB:** | "Chip" DE – Flat @ LOS |
| **LWR:** | 7-8 Yard Cross | **RUB:** | Snap - Pitch – Flat @ LOS |

*The Clipboard*

When we look at pass concepts in these types of offenses, typically when you have a "5-out" type of release (some coaches call this Jailbreak) most coaches are looking to hit the flats. Although this is not always the case, the hope is that the defense is over-aggressive, leaving the flats wide open.

| Set: | Gun T | Team: | Medina |
|---|---|---|---|
| Play: | Lead | Scheme: | Gap |

**Coaches Corner**

With a unique system, Medina ran their "Gun T" offense with great success in 2022, making a big playoff run finishing 11-1.

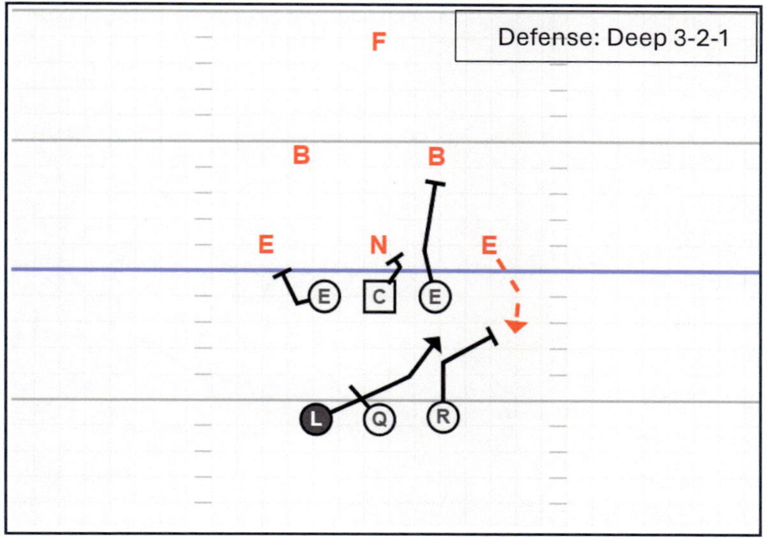


| C: | On (Hook/Seal) | QB: | Handoff to LHB |
|---|---|---|---|
| PSTE: | 2nd Level | LHB: | Read RHB's Block |
| BSTE: | Back Block | RHB: | Kickout PSDE |

*The Clipboard*

The Medina Gun T is simple yet effective, instead of your typical 6-man Sweep, Medina uses a simple "Lead" play to not only try and get their RB's downhill quick, but to help keep their QB involved as a "Pocket passer" that opens up a great play action series!

Jurassic Times

## Coaches Corner

One of the oldest Offensive Systems of its time, Bastrop Tribe is one of the only teams that have been running this system for over a decade.

| Set: | O'Brien | Team: | Bastrop Tribe |
|---|---|---|---|
| Play: | Sweep | Scheme: | Gap |

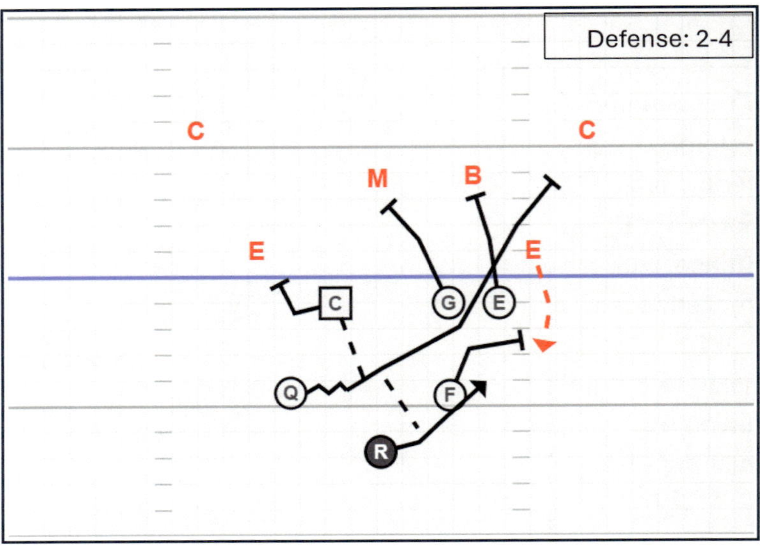


| C: | Back Block | QB: | Motion – Pitch – 2nd Level |
|---|---|---|---|
| G: | 2nd Level | FB: | Kickout PSDE |
| TE: | 2nd Level | RB: | Get downhill – Read FB |

*The Clipboard*

The QB in motion?? The O'Brien system is the only offensive set you'll see move the QB pre-snap in order for him to get a head start on the snap (The Center is aiming for where the RB is lined up, which is in the A Gap). The bread & butter of their offense, Tribe uses every advantage they can to get an extra step on your basic "sweep" play.

## Loraine's Pistol

| Set: | Pistol | Team: | Loraine |
|---|---|---|---|
| Play: | C - Pop | Scheme: | Sweep Pass |

**Coaches Corner**

Everyone has different 6-man "Lingo." Diamond, Bullet, Bone, etc. When a team lines up a back NEXT to AND behind the QB, this is considered "Pistol."

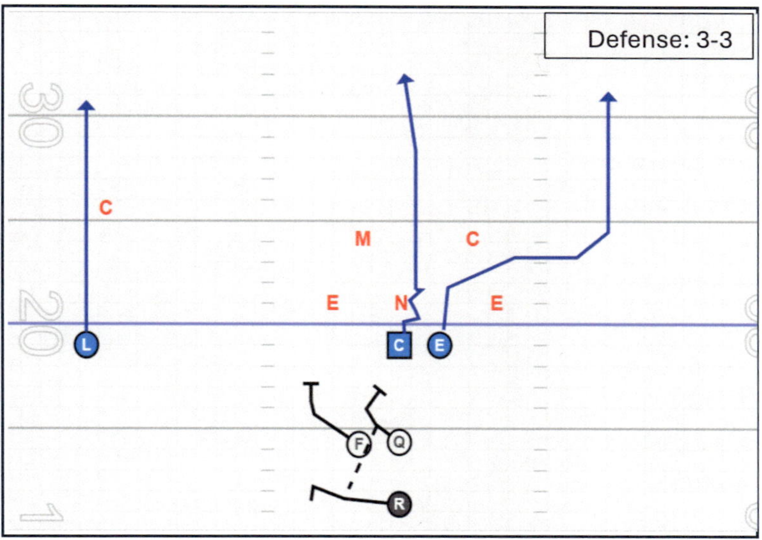


| C: | Chip Delay – Seam | QB: | Pitch – Seal for Backside |
|---|---|---|---|
| TE: | Out & up | FB: | Seal/Hook PSDE (Edge) |
| WR: | M.O.R Fade | RB: | Progression: C - TE |

*The Clipboard*

One of the best ways to counterattack a defense with No defenders over the 10-yard mark – is to attack them with "Middle seams." You Already pull the Mike playside with the sweep action. Now all that's needed is to pull any PSCB who could possibly see the seam route. The Quick "Out & Up" is the perfect way to do that here. The Center is now able to slip behind the Linebackers and find open grass.

To dig a hole, we need a...

| Set: | Tight Trips | Team: | Irion County |
|---|---|---|---|
| Play: | Shovel | Scheme: | Gap/Zone |

## Coaches Corner

In the 11-man world you may have heard or seen a lot of 4x1 sets. Although not a popular set in 6-man, teams will carry this set to gain a numbers advantage.

Defense: 2-4

| C: | Chip – 2nd Level | QB: | Get snap – Ball Out now! |
|---|---|---|---|
| #3 WR: | On (Hook/Seal) | #2 WR: | Step, turn, Ball, Up field |
| #1 WR: | On (Hook/Seal) | RB: | Sell Weakside Sweep |

*The Clipboard*

Just because you're backed up in the Gun, doesn't mean your run game is limited! If you like using WR's in your offense, think of shovels or "tunnel" screens as an extension to your run game. Notice that everyone up front simply follows the same blocking rules! You can use your WR's to complaint your "Hang your hat" run plays.

Use your Up-backs!

**Coaches Corner**

One thing that's a common misconception in many Hybrid or Spread sets is that your Spreadback is the only one that can/needs to be the one that throws! NOPE! Use your Up-Backs!

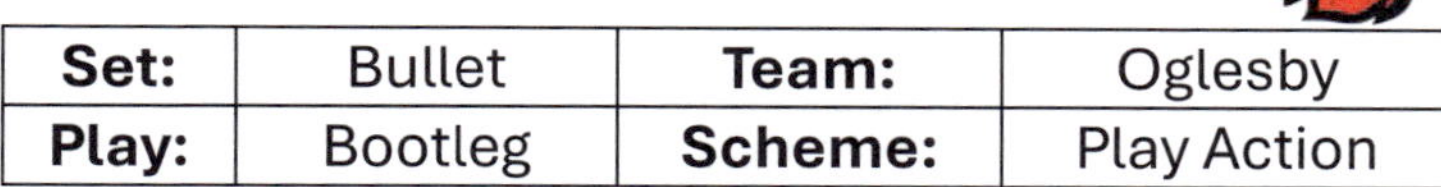

| **Set:** | Bullet | **Team:** | Oglesby |
|---|---|---|---|
| **Play:** | Bootleg | **Scheme:** | Play Action |

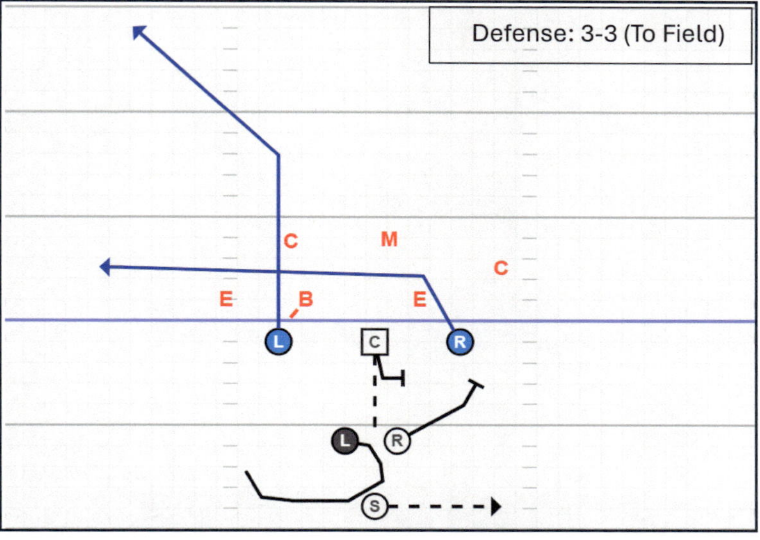


| **C:** | Back – Pass Pro | **SB:** | Sell Sweep |
|---|---|---|---|
| **LWR:** | 7-8 Yard Corner | **LUB:** | Progression: Corner - Drag |
| **RWR:** | 2 Step Drag | **RUB:** | Base Sweep Rules – Block Edge |

*The Clipboard*

When you buy in to using a spread back as your main weapon, you buy in to running sweep to him 10-15 times a game. When you do this, you not only need a way to get the defense to over commit to sweep but a way to save your SB's legs! If you have a QB that you use in other sets but isn't quite a "Spreadback." He is a great piece to put at up-back and run bootleg!

# More Variations

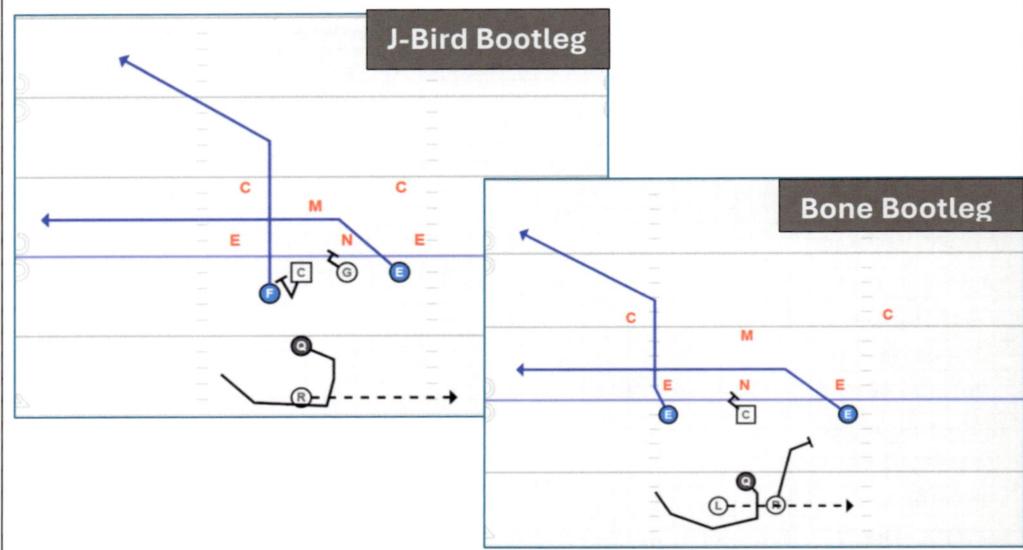

Oglesby vs. Oakwood in the 1A-D2 State Semifinals; *Texas 1A Fan; 2024*

## Coaches Corner

While this play is from 2020, the crack block can be tricky! When taught correctly, your WR can have a lot of fun making this block!

| Set: | J-Gun (F-Split) | Team: | Borden County |
|---|---|---|---|
| Play: | Crack Sweep | Scheme: | Gap |

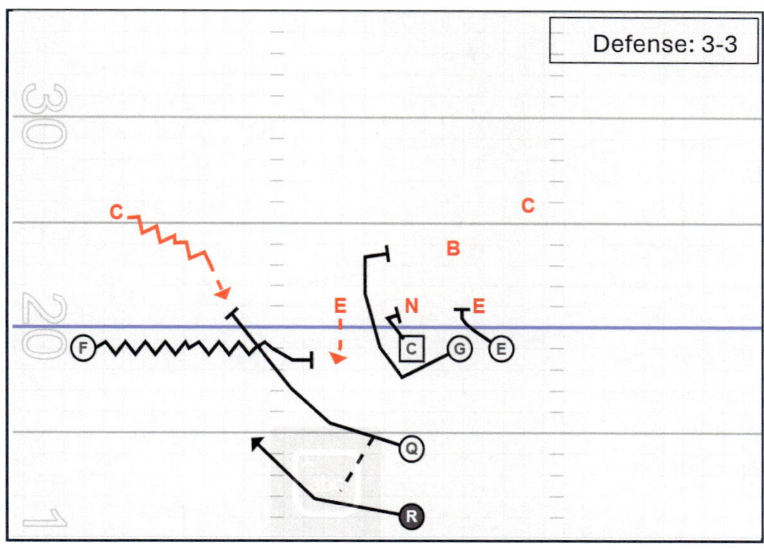


| C: | On (Hook/Seal) | QB: | Pitch – 2nd Level |
|---|---|---|---|
| G: | Skip Pull – 2nd Level | FB: | Motion inside – "Crack" (Seal) PSDE |
| TE: | Scoop/Cut | RB: | Take Pitch – Read QB's Block |

*The Clipboard*

Notice that this is still a "J-Gun" set, but with only one player tagged to move, instead of using 10+ different sets. One thing Borden County did with great success was use the things they were already successful with, and just moved one guy to give the illusion of complexity, while they still ran a simple sweep. They will use the FB's leverage to pin the PSDE inside, instead if kicking him out like they usually would.

# Deja Vu

| Set: | Nasty Bullet | Team: | Rochelle |
|---|---|---|---|
| Play: | 3-Pass | Scheme: | T.B.O |

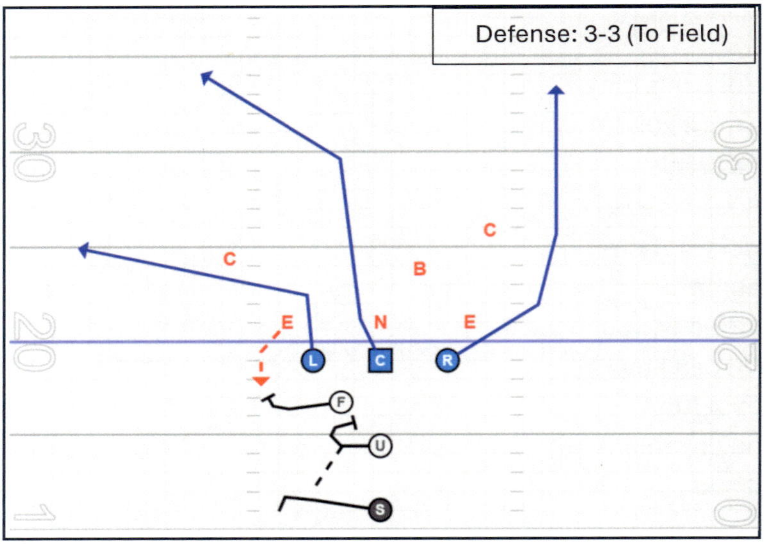

***Coaches Corner***

Rochelle has been an impressive offense over the past 4 years. Averaging 53.4 points a game! Unfortunately, they have been unable to make the playoffs in this 4-year span.

Defense: 3-3 (To Field)

| C: | 10 Yard Corner (Left) | SB: | Progression: Left to Right |
|---|---|---|---|
| LWR: | 3 Step "Flood" Slant | FB: | Hook or Kickout PSDE |
| RWR: | Wide Vertical | UB: | Pitch – Peal for backside |

*The Clipboard*

With many ways to skin a cat, 3-pass can fit into many folds. You can easily build it into a lot of sets you carry, the three routes needed are the Quick Slant, Middle Seam/Corner, and a backside vertical. The main defender you want to put in a bind is the PSCB. The goal here is to vertically stretch him, to help your SB make an easy read.

## Round peg into a square hole

| Set: | Gun T (Split) | Team: | Whitharral |
|---|---|---|---|
| Play: | Flood | Scheme: | Sweep Pass |

**Coaches Corner**

If you were to watch a full Whitharral game. You would say "Wow those plays look so similar to 11-man" It's because they are! And they are very successful with it!

Defense: 4-2 Strong

| C: | 2 Step Drag | QB: | Pitch – Block BSDE/Edge |
|---|---|---|---|
| LTE: | 7-8 Yard Corner | FB: | Seal or Kickout PSDE |
| RTE: | On (Hook/Seal) | RB: | Progression: Corner - Drag |

*The Clipboard*

One of the most "Motion" heavy teams in the State, Whitharral are the kings of "Few plays, many ways." They can get to their Sweep series in tons of ways, and here they split out of one their top athletes and get him moving! Giving him a running start on the defense. This motion could also cause an "early" run fit trigger from the PSCB which might open up the corner route even more.

# Open that Screen Door

| Set: | J-Gun (Split) | Team: | Gordon |
|---|---|---|---|
| Play: | Slip Screen | Scheme: | Screen |

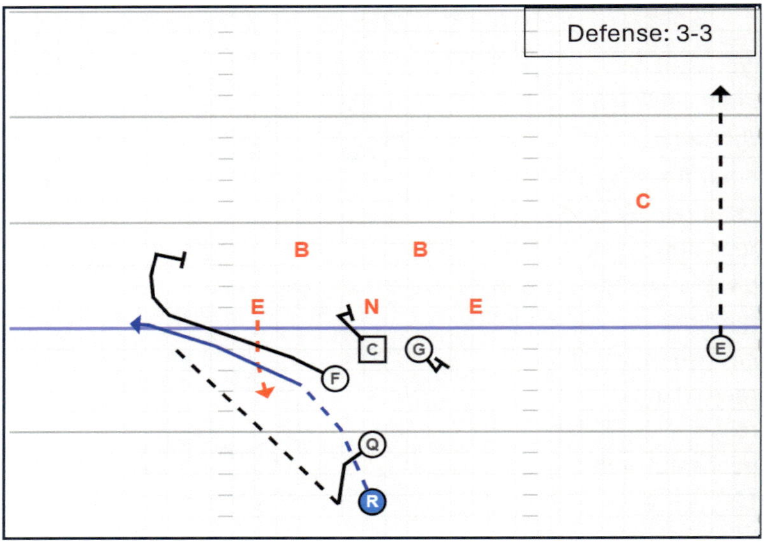

**Coaches Corner**

Creating quite the dynasty and winning back-to-back State championships. Gordon has won 30 straight games. In 29 of which they have "45'ed" their opponent.

Defense: 3-3

| C: | On (Hook/Seal) | QB: | Token Fake – Slight hesitation – Dump to RB |
|---|---|---|---|
| G: | Pass Pro – Backside Edge | FB: | Initially miss PSDE – "Bait" & wait for LB |
| WR: | Decoy Fade | RB: | Token Fake – Flat behind LOS |

*The Clipboard*

One of the most forgotten players in a play action series, is the person we just faked to...the running back! Another great "Complaint to the complaint play!" The key here is for the QB to give the slight hesitation of a "Shot play" and get any BSLB's or safety's drawn away from the screen side. You want to make it as easy as possible for the FB "waiting for the bait" on his block.

## Plano Pop Pass

| Set: | Pistol | Team: | Coram Deo |
|---|---|---|---|
| Play: | TE – Pop | Scheme: | Drop Back |

**Coaches Corner**

A perfect example of "it's not how you start; it's how you finish." Coram Deo started the 2024 season 3-4 yet were able to make it all the way to the state championship!

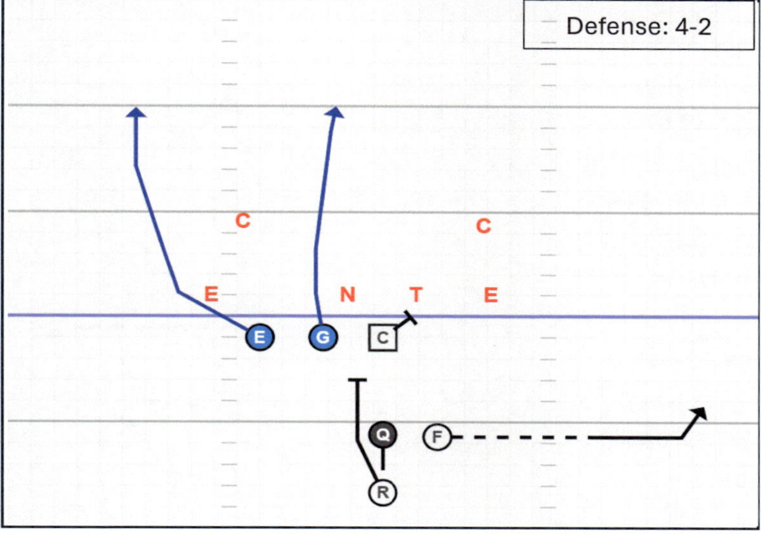


| C: | Pass pro – Backside A Gap | QB: | Progression: Pop – Wide Vert |
|---|---|---|---|
| G: | 3 Step Middle "Pop" Route | FB: | Checkdown Swing |
| TE: | Wide Vertical | RB: | Pass pro – Playside A Gap |

*The Clipboard*

Another one that I personally coached against last year! I was impressed how simple Plano (Coram Deo) made this play. When in their Pistol set, most of the time they ran sweep. But instead of worrying about the typical Play action, they instead would step back as fast as possible and get the ball out! Hoping that your defense will overreact to sweep once again!

"Be the Hammer, not the Nail"

**Coaches Corner**

Some coaches believe that running typical tight plays like Hammer and weak sweep with wider angles come easier when backed up in Gun.

| **Set:** | J-Gun | **Team:** | Throckmorton |
|---|---|---|---|
| **Play:** | Hammer | **Scheme:** | Gap |

Defense: Deep 3-2-1

| **C:** | Back Block | **QB:** | Pitch – 2nd Level |
|---|---|---|---|
| **G:** | On (Hook/Seal) | **FB:** | Pull – Kickout PSDE |
| **TE:** | 2nd Level | **RB:** | 1 Sidestep – Get Downhill |

*The Clipboard*

Whether this is something you add on as a mix-up to your Tight offense, or you see this as a set you'd like to base out of. The big positive that I see running sweep out of base hybrid sets (like J-Gun) is that you create a fast way to get downhill ASAP. With the RB being as deep as 8-10 yards, he can almost take no horizontal steps and has a downhill track almost immediately. The obvious negative to these sets is the lack of run game creativity.

***Coaches Corner***

**Scissors** = A Post route with a corner route coming underneath.

**Mesh** = Two drag routes that cross each together, typically against man coverages.

| **Set:** | J-Gun | **Team:** | Buena Vista |
|---|---|---|---|
| **Play:** | Scissors + Mesh | **Scheme:** | Play Action |

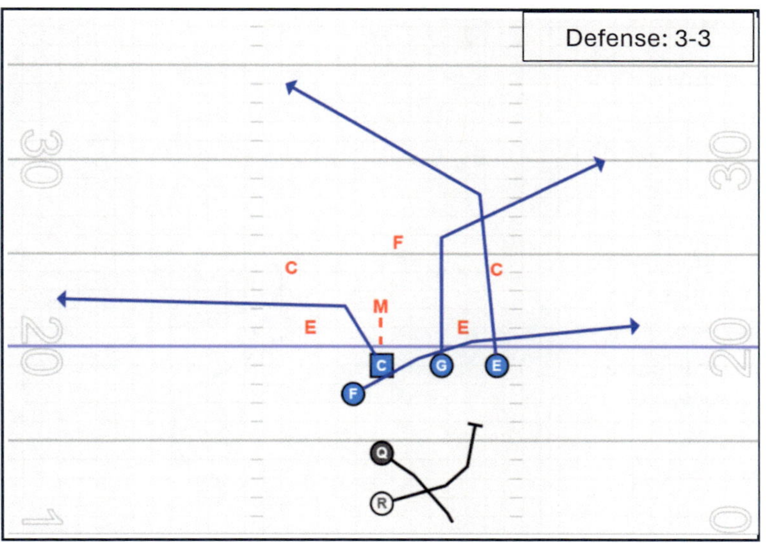


| **C:** | 2 Yard Drag | **QB:** | Progression: Post – Corner - Drags |
|---|---|---|---|
| **G:** | 5-6 Yard Corner | **FB:** | Flat Drag @ LOS |
| **TE:** | 8-10 Yard Post | **RB:** | Sweep path – protect Edge |

*The Clipboard*

There are ways to pair concepts together for the right reason, but in 6-man football we absolutely have no time to ask our athletes to go through 3-4 progressions. We can make this progression in two ways:

**1 High Safety:** Corner – Flats (F-C)

**No Safety's:** Post – Flats (C-F)

## Bend it like Blackwell

***Coaches Corner***

Something that is considered "uncommon" in 6-Man is straight up handoffs from Gun preferred to a sweep. Most teams will use handoffs for their misdirection only.

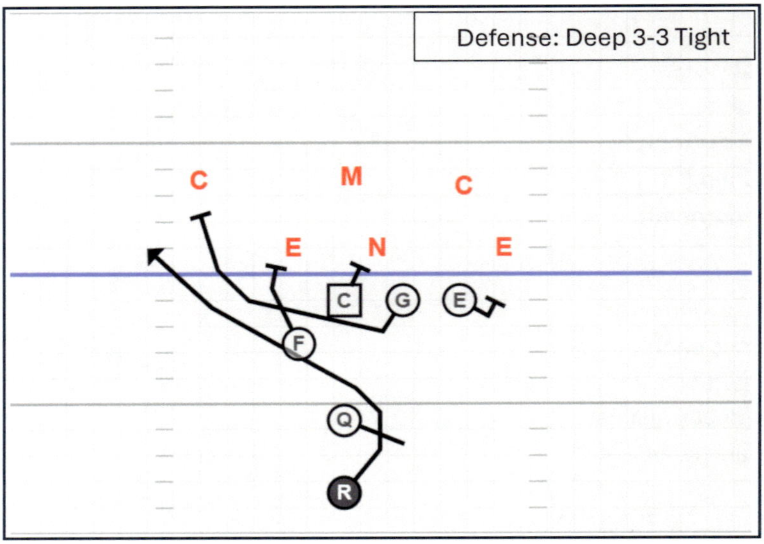

| **Set:** | J-Gun | **Team:** | Blackwell |
|---|---|---|---|
| **Play:** | Bend G-Lead | **Scheme:** | Gap |

Defense: Deep 3-3 Tight

| **C:** | Down | **QB:** | Handoff (Like it's Lead) |
|---|---|---|---|
| **G:** | Pull & Kickout Edge | **FB:** | Down - On |
| **TE:** | Back Block | **RB:** | Start on "Lead" path – Then bounce & read G's block |

*The Clipboard*

If you are a "Handoff guru" and have Lead as a staple in your offense, then you absolutely need "Bend Lead" in your arsenal. A very easy to teach scheme, this will be disguised to the defense as it will look exactly like lead as it's hitting downhill, unless a LB's eyes is keyed on the pulling Guard.

## “That’s a McCool RPO”

***Coaches Corner***

Although Texas has 300+ schools playing 6-man throughout UIL & TAPPS. 6-Man football was actually invented in Chester, Nebraska in 1934.

| Set: | Empty DBL Wing | Team: | McCool Junction (NE) |
|---|---|---|---|
| Play: | Sweep R.P.O | Scheme: | Gap |

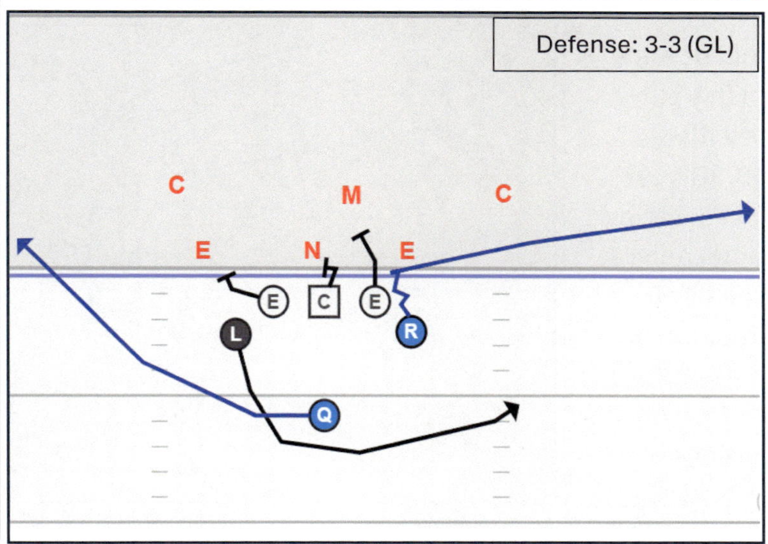


| C: | On (Hook/Seal) | QB: | Handoff to LHB |
|---|---|---|---|
| BSTE: | Back Block | LHB: | Handoff behind QB – Read Edge |
| PSTE: | 2nd Level | RHB: | 2 Second Chip & Delay - Flat |

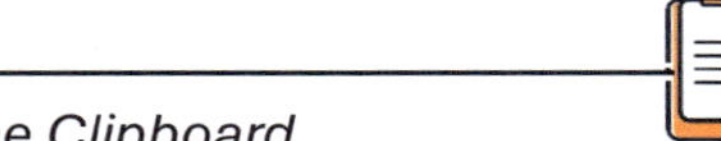

*The Clipboard*

**A Nebraska School!** Digging through film, I stumbled upon a 2019 State Championship game and found a very cool Short Yardage idea from McCool Junction. Starting with a shift, they give a handoff to their RB acting on a sweep action. But he then has the option to throw the flat route depending how aggressive the PSDE is. There is even a “emergency” route backside with the QB trailing to the front pylon.

**Coaches Corner**

Patience is key on this play as well the QB/SB's eyes. The FB (delay route) must wait till all other routes almost cross his face before getting flat.

| Set: | J-Gun | Team: | Klondike |
|---|---|---|---|
| Play: | Flood - Under | Scheme: | T.B.O |

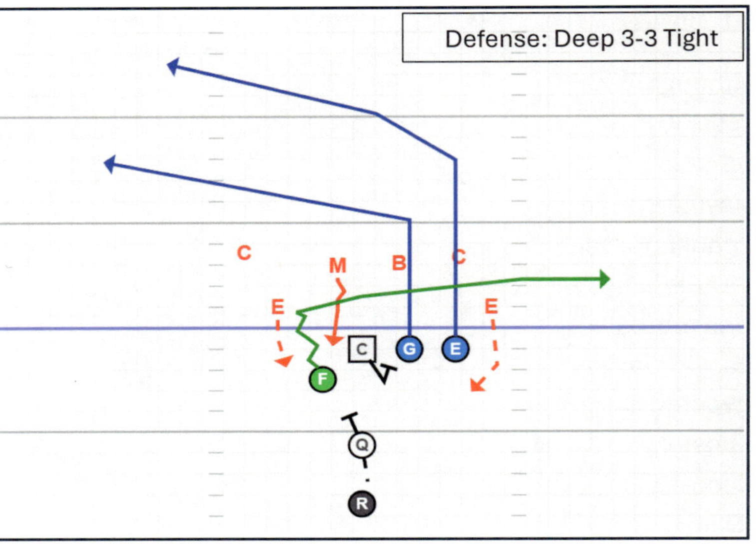


| C: | Pass Pro – A Gap | QB: | Pitch to RB – Pass Pro A Gap |
|---|---|---|---|
| G: | 5 Yard Slant | FB: | 2 second delay – Underneath Drag |
| TE: | 8-10 Yard Cross | RB: | Progression: Slant - Under |

*The Clipboard*

A very common defense in 6-man is "man" coverage. One of the best "Man Beaters" you can carry on your call sheet is any sort of "clear out" concept. These typically work better from compressed hybrid sets, thus hiding the player who is running your delayed under route. I have also seen this play designed to the Center & Tight End.

**Coaches Corner**

The Cinderella Story of the 2024 season. Starting out at 2-5, Oakwood went on a 7-game winning streak to make it the 1A-D2 Championship game.

| Set: | Bullet Twins | Team: | Oakwood |
|---|---|---|---|
| Play: | Weak Sweep | Scheme: | Gap |

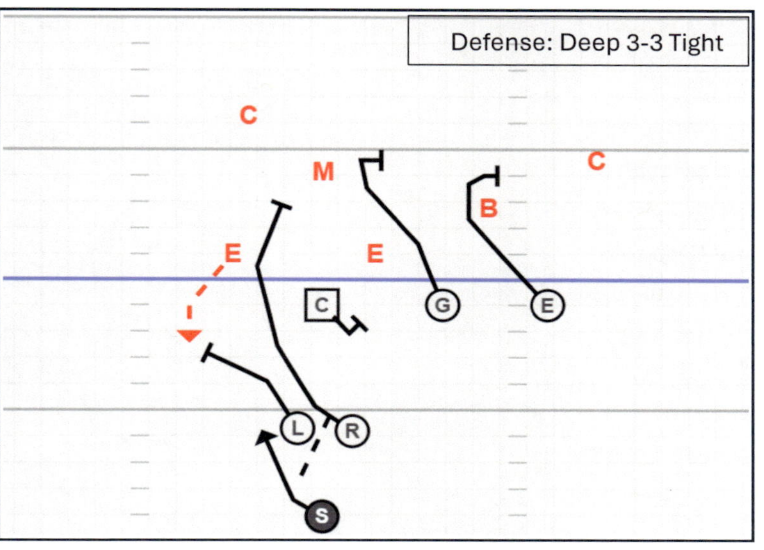


| C: | Back Block | SB: | Get downhill asap – Read UB's block |
|---|---|---|---|
| G: | 2nd Level | LUB: | Kickout PSDE |
| TE: | 2nd Level | RUB: | Take Snap – 2nd Level |

*The Clipboard*

Always have a weakside answer! While this scheme works just fine from Bullet, remember to keep one thing in mind! There is no one to "down" block the weakside A gap here. You can still absolutely run this play with great success, but this is a play where you will need to give your Spreadback an "Opposite" audible call for him to make if he sees this "un-blockable" look.

## Why not Both?

| Set: | Tight Trips | Team: | Miami |
|---|---|---|---|
| Play: | Sweep Option | Scheme: | Sweep Pass |

Defense: 2-2-2

### Coaches Corner

Finally! A 6-man RPO! The easiest way to run any sort of true RPO in 6-man, is to tag a same side “Flood” type route when you run sweep.

| C: | Back Block | SB: | Progression: Read PSCB |
|---|---|---|---|
| G: | Down | FB: | Deep Cross (Opposite pylon) |
| TE: | 3 Step Whip route | UB: | Snap & Pitch – Kickout or Seal Edge |

*The Clipboard*

One of the greatest things you can attach to your sweep is a single route that isolates one defender. We now create the favorite 11-man coaches’ buzz word... RPO! We create a simple option like type scenario, where we now have made an easy read for our spread back. CB’s plays whip route = **RUN**. CB plays soft coverage or commits to sweep = **Throw Whip!** We are vertically stretching the Playside Cornerback and making him “wrong” no matter what!

**Coaches Corner**

It's important to remember to teach your QB/SB that situational awareness is very important. If the drag is normally our first read – on 4th & long, we want to look at deeper routes first.

| **Set:** | J-Gun | **Team:** | Nazareth |
|---|---|---|---|
| **Play:** | Flood + Cross | **Scheme:** | T.B.O |

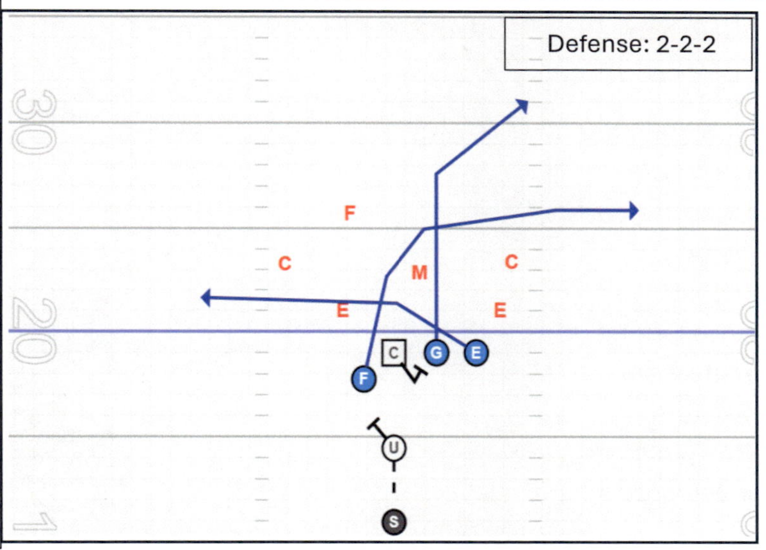


| **C:** | Pass Pro – A Gap | **SB:** | Progression: Corner - Cross |
|---|---|---|---|
| **G:** | 7-8 Yard Corner | **FB:** | 5-6 Yard Cross |
| **TE:** | 2 Yard Drag | **UB:** | Pitch – Pass Pro Edge |

*The Clipboard*

Although I have put a lot of teams in this section who base in Hybrid sets, I wanted to show an example of a team who prefers to be in tight rather than Hybrid or spread. But when in a 4th & long situation, they pull out J-Gun and base it around their best athlete. What makes this concept special is the stress it puts on the leverage of a 1-high safety. The Corner route attacks the outside hip of the safety, forcing him to have his eves on either the corner or the cross.

| Set: | Wing Gun | Team: | Benjamin |
|---|---|---|---|
| Play: | Trap - Wheel | Scheme: | T.B.O |

**Coaches Corner**

Always remember that everyone is eligible in your offense, meaning we can get really creative and even turn TRAP pulls into wheel routes!

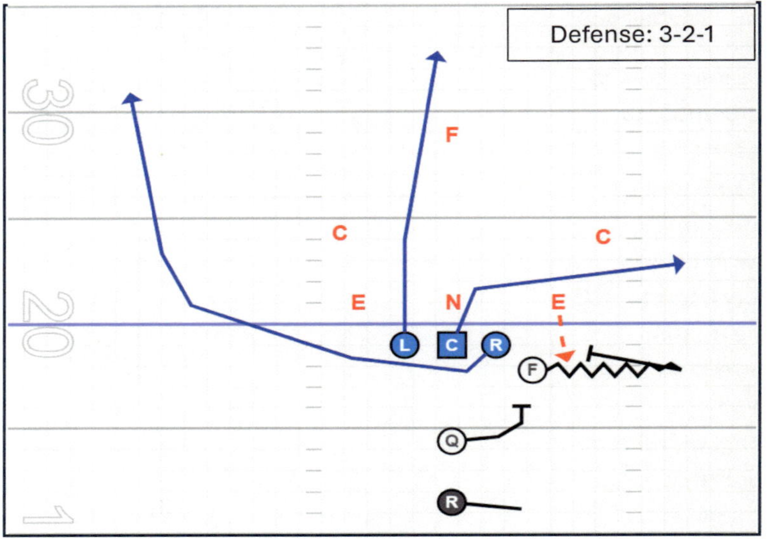


| C: | Slant/Flat | QB: | Pitch – Pass Pro Backside |
|---|---|---|---|
| LTE: | Pipe/Seam | FB: | Short motion outside – Crack Hook/Seal PSDE |
| RTE: | Trap Pull – Get wide & Vertical | RB: | Progression: Flat – Pipe - Wheel |

*The Clipboard*

We've seen a couple versions of 3-pass already in this book. And this might be the most creative version of it so far! Starting with some window dressing, the FB is brought in for a sweep crack! If you notice, Benjamin keeps the same base rules for 3-pass. A Slant (Center), A Pipe/Seam (backside TE), And a Backside wheel (From the Playside TE)! Creativity comes in simple formulas; all you need is one tag!

# Hide the TE

| Set: | Empty - Stacked FB | Team: | Gordon |
|---|---|---|---|
| Play: | Post - Iso | Scheme: | Play Action |

**Coaches Corner**

**Defensive perspective** = Flipping sides of the ball, it's important to always teach your DBs to never let a motion suck you into the backfield. The QB is dead = DE's have him.

Defense: 4-2

| C: | Pass Pro – A Gap | QB: | Token Fake sweep – Throw Post |
|---|---|---|---|
| BSTE: | 5-6 Yard Quick Post | FB: | Pass Pro – Weakside A Gap |
| PSTE: | Pass Pro - Edge | RB: | Motion behind QB – Fake Sweep |

*The Clipboard*

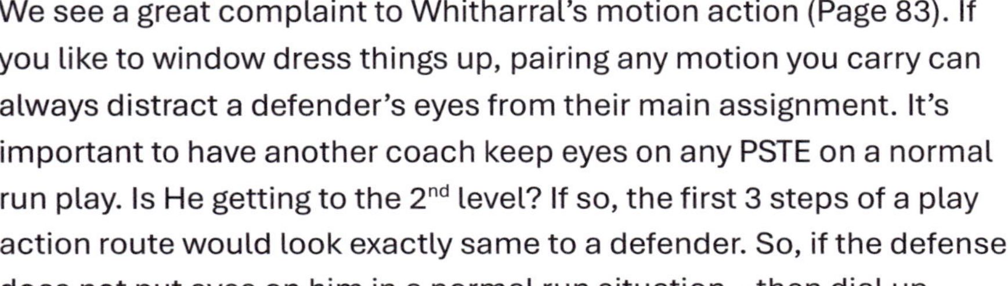

We see a great complaint to Whitharral's motion action (Page 83). If you like to window dress things up, pairing any motion you carry can always distract a defender's eyes from their main assignment. It's important to have another coach keep eyes on any PSTE on a normal run play. Is He getting to the 2nd level? If so, the first 3 steps of a play action route would look exactly same to a defender. So, if the defense does not put eyes on him in a normal run situation – then dial up something for him later in the game!

A Happy Eye

| Set: | Hybrid Eye | Team: | Happy |
|---|---|---|---|
| Play: | Speed Option | Scheme: | Gap/Zone |

Coaches Corner

6-man is full of "Iron-man" players. Guys that can play multiple positions – so try not to fit one kid into one filter. Find creative ways to move your personal around!

Defense: 2-3-1

| C: | 2nd level | QB: | Read PSCB |
|---|---|---|---|
| WR: | Decoy Hitch | FB: | Snap – Pitch – Seal PSDE |
| TE: | Back Block | RB: | 4 x 4 Yard Spacing |

*The Clipboard*

**Technically** this is defined as a tight set. But Happy uses great creativity with putting their QB in a position to succeed. Instead, of a basic tight set, they use their FB here as a "Middle Man." Happy will use these in many ways, their favorite run play from it is a speed option (Like seen here), but they will also use lots of T.B.O concepts from it, that can feel like more of a traditional drop-back series with the pocket their pass protection creates.

QR Code is everything Happy does out of this set.

# Spread

A Spread set can sometimes sound like a broad term. As truly there are many different styles of the Spread system in 6-man football. The simplest way to define a spread formation is if the offense has 2 or more Receivers.

It is possible for there to be different kinds of spread offenses. Traditionally it is how the Quarterback/Spreadback is used.

## Traditional Quarterback.

Teams who want more of a "Pocket" passing type Quarterback, will usually run Shogun sets where the RB(s) is offset to the side of the quarterback and usually will not include a lot "second exchanges." We have referred to these sets as "Pro Style" spread offenses. Some teams will even use this method in a true "Empty" set. With 4 WR's at the Line of scrimmage.

Allen Academy in a "Gun Pro" Set

Covenant Classical in a 3x1 Empty Set

## Spreadback Style

If you have never heard of the term "Spreadback" in 6-man, the easiest way to describe this player is as "**THE** Athlete," essentially the player who can throw, run and is just generally a jack of all trades.

In these types of sets with a Spreadback, most teams will line him up about 12-15 yards back from the line of scrimmage. With an Up-back (in front of the SB) about 6-7 yards from the Center. This type of system usually involves a ton of second exchanges, making the Spreadback eligible to run if needed.

Robert Lee using a Spreadback in a "Diamond Twins" set

Extra Page for Notes & Diagrams

Extra Page for Notes & Diagrams

# Wheel's off

| Set: | Diamond Twins | Team: | Cherokee |
|---|---|---|---|
| Play: | Post/Wheel | Scheme: | T.B.O |

**Coaches Corner**

**Note from Flim Clip:**

Even though this is an offensive book, I liked the idea of the PSDE "Jamming" & rerouting the Slot's route.

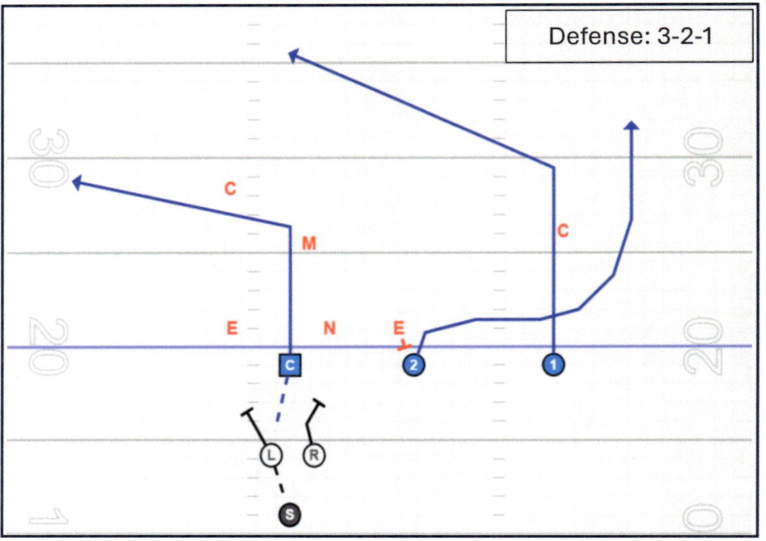


| C: | Deep Slant (7-8 Yards) | SB: | Progression: C – Post-Wheel |
|---|---|---|---|
| #2 WR: | Out & Up Wheel | LUB: | Snap – Pitch – Pass Pro Left |
| #1 WR: | 10-12 Yard Post | RUB: | Pass Pro Right |

*The Clipboard*

One of the most important things to note in this concept here, is the deep Center slant. This helps open the post route a lot, as it keeps the CB flat footed and keeps him from staying away from any kind of "Deep zone." A great pairing with the Post is the "Out & up" route by the wheel, which typically can find a lot of open grass, the CB is forced to follow the Post or stay on his Island.

# "Spread Right and Spread Left"

## *Coaches Corner*

Going 11-man in 2024. Hill Country ran the Diamond as their base offense for nearly a decade. Averaging 45.2 points a game over this stretch.

| **Set:** | Diamond | **Team:** | Austin Hill Country |
|---|---|---|---|
| **Play:** | "Spread" | **Scheme:** | Sweep Read |

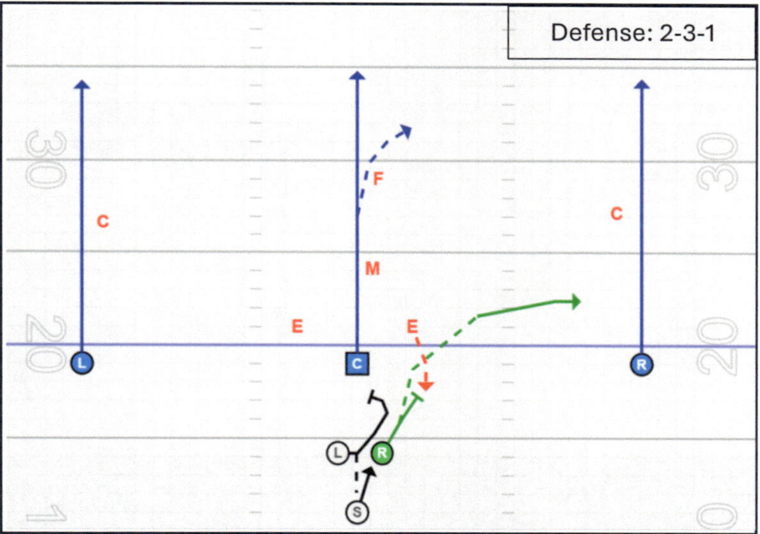


| **C:** | Seam | **SB:** | Get downhill now! |
|---|---|---|---|
| **RWR:** | M.O.R Fade | **LUB:** | Snap – Pitch – Peal Backside |
| **LWR:** | M.O.R Fade | **RUB:** | Read PSDE: Block or Dump |

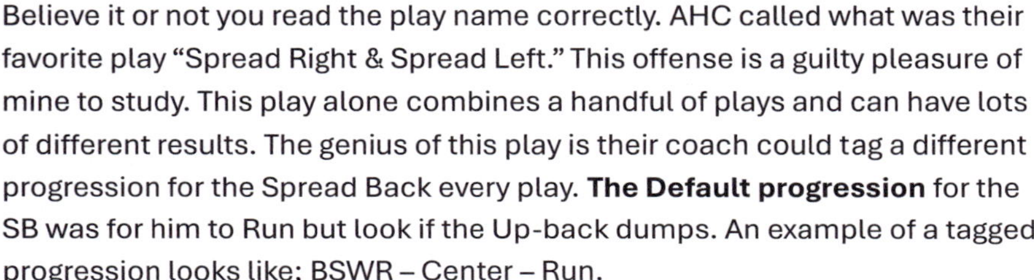

*The Clipboard*

Believe it or not you read the play name correctly. AHC called what was their favorite play "Spread Right & Spread Left." This offense is a guilty pleasure of mine to study. This play alone combines a handful of plays and can have lots of different results. The genius of this play is their coach could tag a different progression for the Spread Back every play. **The Default progression** for the SB was for him to Run but look if the Up-back dumps. An example of a tagged progression looks like; BSWR – Center – Run.

# More Variations

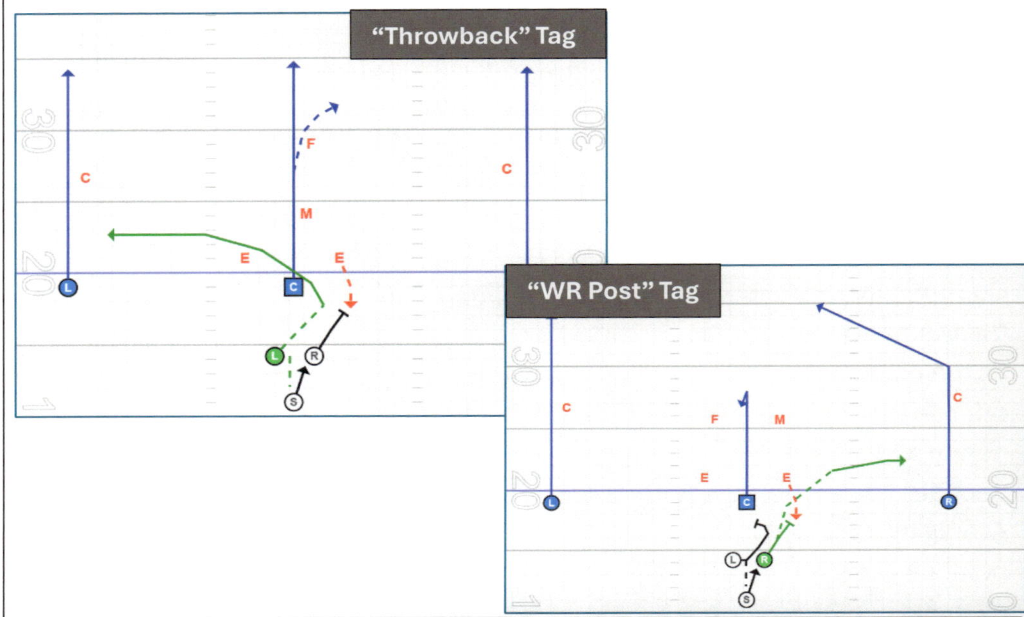

Water Valley vs. Rankin; *Texas 1A Fan; 2024*

## Start Your Engines

| Set: | Diamond | Team: | Milford |
|---|---|---|---|
| Play: | SB Draw | Scheme: | Cross Block |

**Coaches Corner**

In 2018, on their run to the State championship game. Milford's Spread back ran for 1600+ Yards while passing for 2000+ Yards.

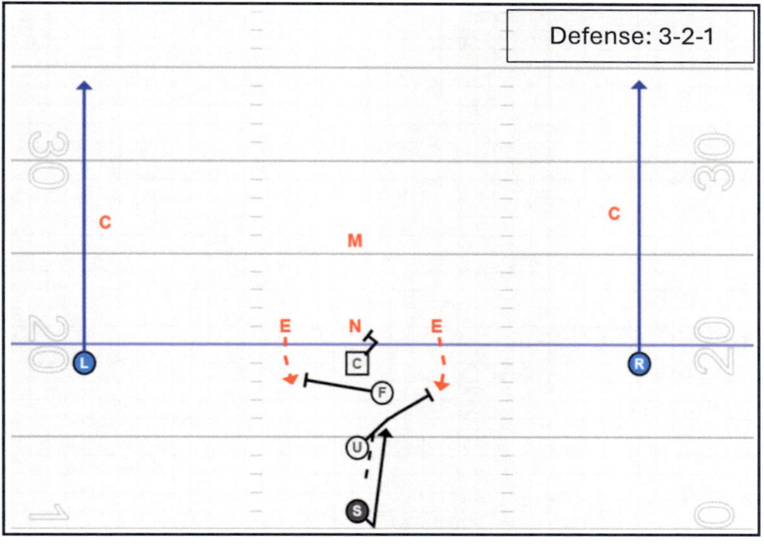


| C: | On (Hook/Seal) | SB: | One step back – Get downhill |
|---|---|---|---|
| LWR: | M.O.R Fade | FB: | Kickout BSDE |
| RWR: | M.O.R Fade | UB: | Snap – Pitch – Kickout PSDE |

*The Clipboard*

Typically, in most 2 WR spread sets seen nowadays with a traditional spread back. Most teams are excepting intermediate to deep developing pass concepts. Perfect way to punish a defense for this? Let the Ends over commit and get your 4.6 spread back downhill now!

When you get the opportunity to have a talented spread back, remember that the ball will be in his hands 50-60 times a game. Find ways to keep his legs fresh!

Mike Leach would be Proud

| Set: | Empty Stack | Team: | Covenant Classical |
|---|---|---|---|
| Play: | Fade/Out | Scheme: | Drop Back |

## Coaches Corner

Something that is common in a lot of 6-man defenses is coaches will typically only send one rusher since the QB is "Dead."

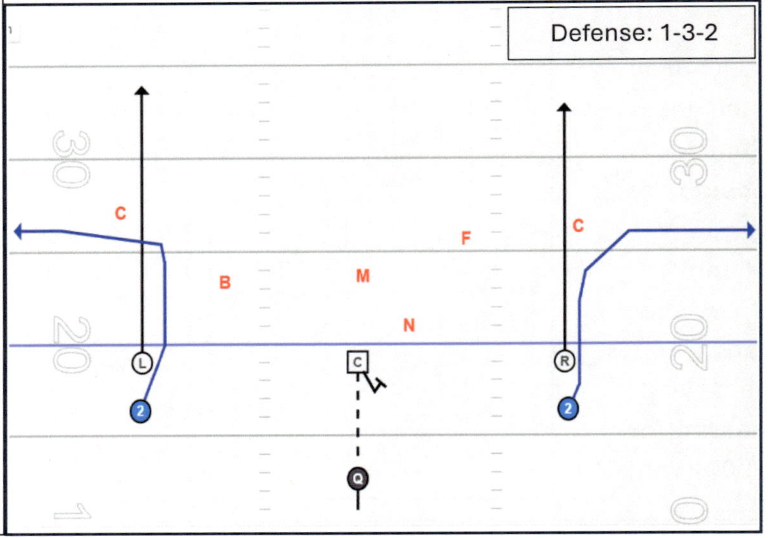


| C: | Pass Pro | QB: | Progression: Best Leverage |
|---|---|---|---|
| LWR: | M.O.R Fade | #2 WR's: | 7-8 Rolled Speed Out |
| RWR: | M.O.R Fade | - | |

*The Clipboard*

Although a six-man Defensive coordinator's first thoughts might be, "Empty? The QB is dead and has almost no pass protection." While maybe there's some truth to this, if you can draw up some simple concepts – you have **5 vertical threats** at the line of scrimmage! Taking advantage of leverage is something that can be overlooked by coaches a lot. With soft inside leverage given by the CB's, we can basically get "free yards" with a quick out to the WR's.

Eye Candy

**Coaches Corner**

On Deeper "Out" routes, I always found an important coaching point is to have the WR "Round" the top of the route instead of chopping his feet down on his cut.

| **Set:** | Spread - Bone | **Team:** | Whitharral |
|---|---|---|---|
| **Play:** | P.A Option | **Scheme:** | Play Action |

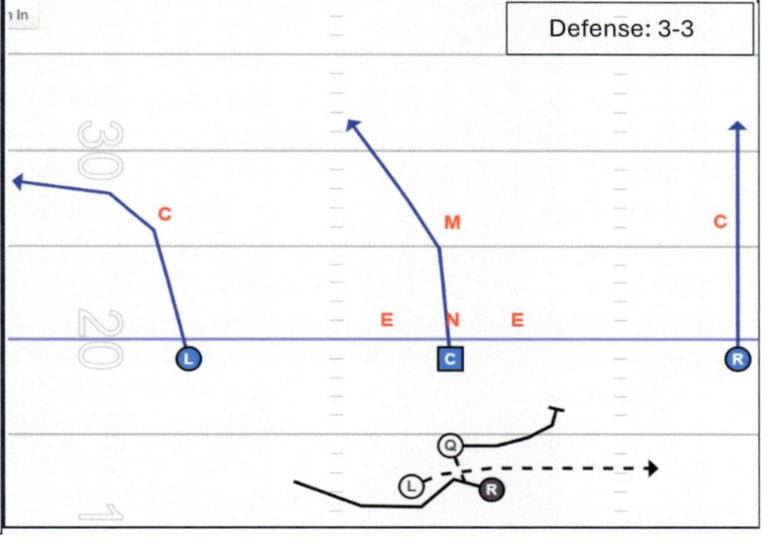


| **C:** | "Bending" Seam | **QB:** | Pitch to RB – Hook/Seal BSDE |
|---|---|---|---|
| **LWR:** | 10-12 Yard Deep Out | **LHB:** | Sell "Sweep" Handoff |
| **RWR:** | M.O.R Fade | **RHB:** | Progression: Out-Seam-Run |

*The Clipboard*

To say seeing this play intrigued me, is an understatement. If you have trouble understanding the play diagram, completely understandable! We first get a true first pitch exchange with the Right RB. The LHB now takes a wide sweep path like he's getting the handoff (Think 11-Man's power read). The right RB proceeds to fake said handoff and now can either run or throw the "Flood" concept.

**Coaches Corner**

A certain verbiage we use for any kind of 3 WR set, we call "Ruby.'" (Diamond with only 1 Up-Back).

| Set: | Ruby | Team: | Avalon |
|---|---|---|---|
| Play: | Speed Option | Scheme: | Zone |

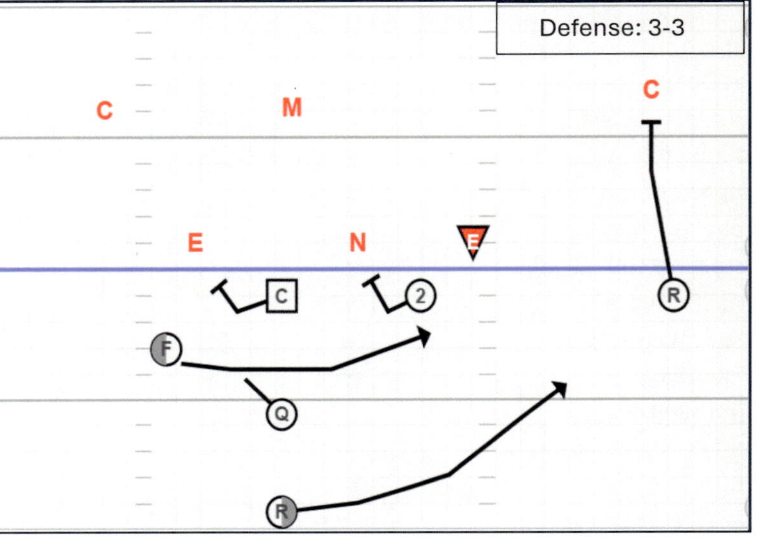


| C: | Down Block | QB: | Handoff to FB |
|---|---|---|---|
| #2 WR: | Down/Crack NG | FB: | Read PSDE – Keep or Pitch to RB |
| RWR: | Stalk Block | RB: | 4 x 4 Yard Spacing |

*The Clipboard*

The typical spread offense stereotype is that it's harder to run the ball when in a spread formation, this is not always the case! If you move a "slot" WR deep enough into the backfield, you can find ways to use him in your run game. Whether this be a shovel, tunnel screen, or getting him involved in the sweep series with an option action! Find your 2nd best athlete on the field and have a call for him in every type of series you have.

# More Variations

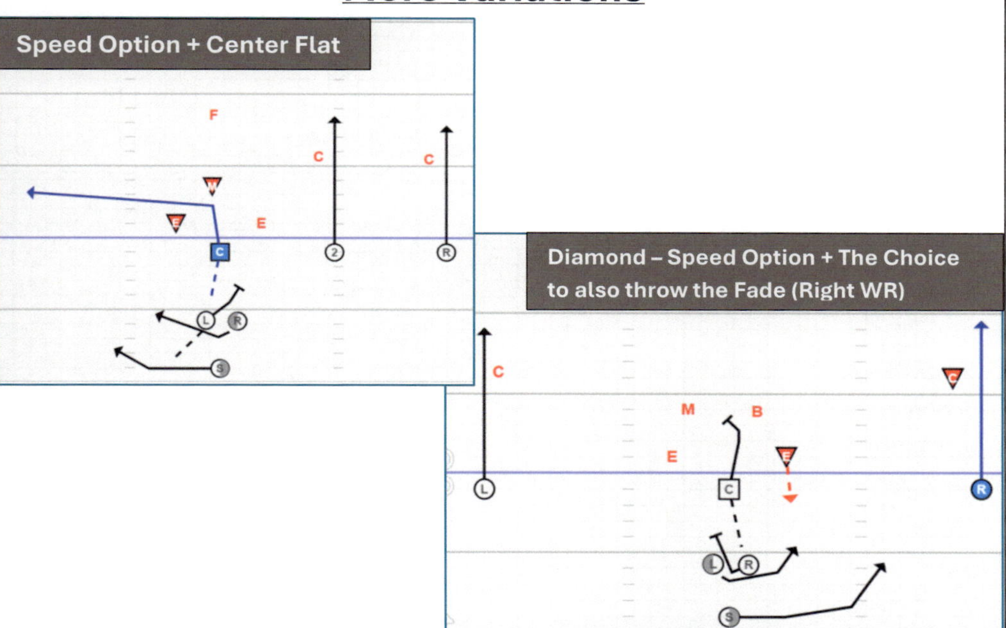

Hermleigh vs. Loraine; *Texas 1A Fan; 2024*

It's a Jailbreak!

**Coaches Corner**

A "Jailbreak" is the most popular type of T.B.O. It typically involves all 5 receiving threats releasing into a route. Usually with 3 vertical routes and 2 flats.

| Set: | Pro | Team: | Bracken Christian |
|---|---|---|---|
| Play: | Jailbreak | Scheme: | T.B.O |

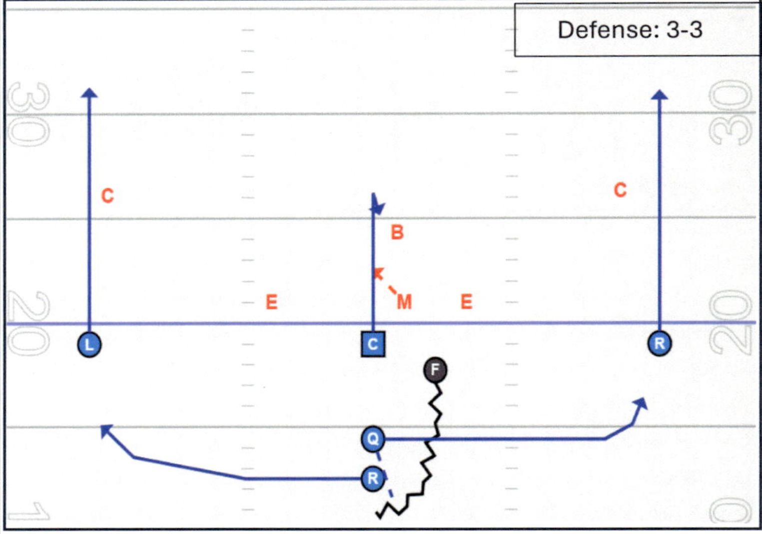


| C: | 10 Yard Curl | QB: | Snap – Pitch – Flat/Swing Right |
|---|---|---|---|
| LWR: | M.O.R Fade | FB: | Motion behind RB – Read #'s advantage |
| RWR: | M.O.R Fade | RB: | Flat/Swing Left |

*The Clipboard*

With "Jailbreak" the typical progression rules for your spread back are slightly different then your typical passing concept. But it's very simple! One of the reasons this has been such a popular T.B.O in any offensive set is that if the defense sends 2+ rushers, you are stretching the defense so horizontally, that someone is bound to be open! If the defense only sends one rusher, then you want your spread back to **RUN!**

# More Variations

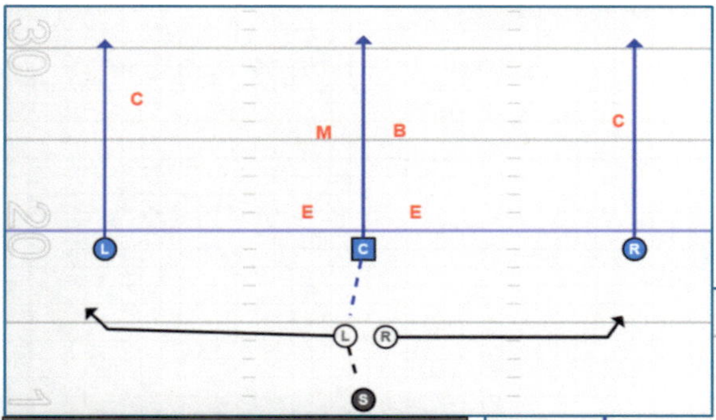

Diamond - Jailbreak

Diamond – Jailbreak Switch

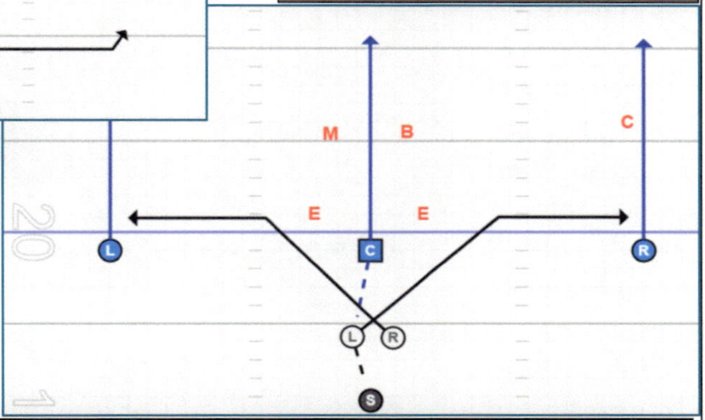

Gordon vs. Jonesboro in the 1A-D1 State Quarterfinals; *Texas 1A Fan 2024*

## Spreading Short Yardage

### Coaches Corner

**MOTION AS LEVERAGE!** I will sound like a broken record saying this, but there is nothing wrong with using a player's movement to get him in a better position as a lead blocker!

| Set: | Ruby | Team: | Springlake-Earth |
|---|---|---|---|
| Play: | Sweep | Scheme: | Zone |

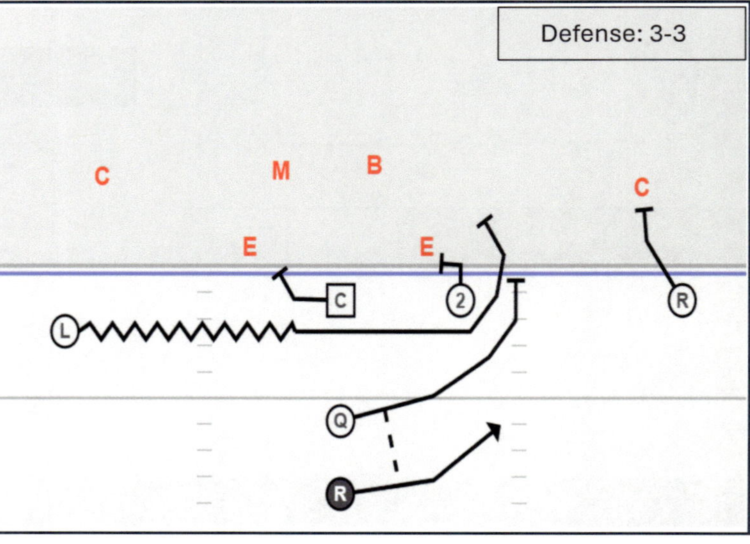


| C: | Back Block | QB: | Pitch – 2nd Level |
|---|---|---|---|
| LWR: | Motion – Lead to 2nd Level | #2 WR: | Crack (Hook/Seal) PSDE |
| RWR: | Stalk Block | RB: | Get wide – Read QB's block |

*The Clipboard*

For you spread guys, I had to get a short yardage play in here for y'all! It is an easy thing to say, "Inside the 5, just go tight!" But one can certainly understand the need to stay in your base offense, to not tip your hand all game. We once again see motion being used to gain a leverage advantage! It's important to note that Springlake-Earth times the motion up perfectly as the WR gets right on the Center's hip!

Read it or Weep

Coaches Corner

A Route I wanted to mention that shouldn't be forgotten here, is the backside flat route by the center! I don't think this should be a primary read. But I do think you can tag this for when you want it thrown!

| Set: | Diamond | Team: | Knox City |
|---|---|---|---|
| Play: | Flood Option | Scheme: | Sweep Read |

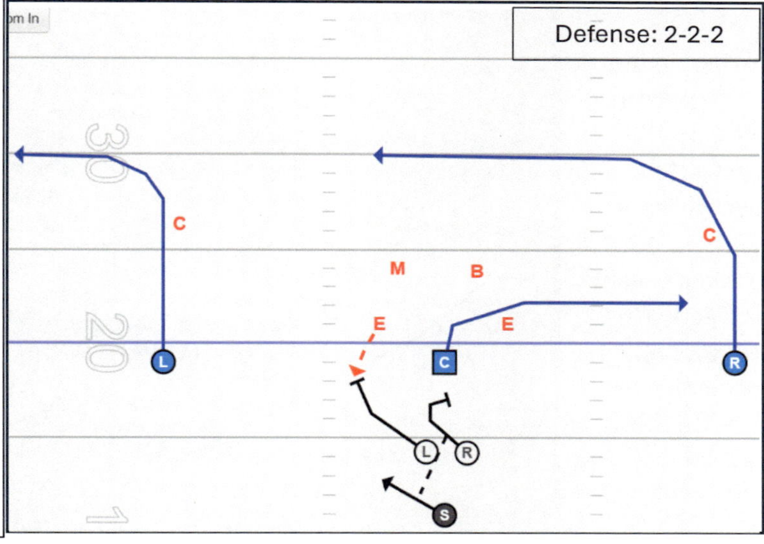


| C: | Backside Flat | SB: | Progression: Out – Dig - Run |
|---|---|---|---|
| LWR: | 10-12 Yard Deep Out | LUB: | Kickout or Hook/Seal PSDE |
| RWR: | 10-12 Yard Speed Dig | RUB: | Snap – Pitch – Seal BSDE |

*The Clipboard*

My Favorite kind of sweeps to see from spread sets are ones that attach routes on them as well. Cause why make your WR's block when they can possibly be thrown too? While pairing plays like this, make sure you make these easy and "throwable" reads. Obviously, we wouldn't tag the PSWR on a Post route. But we always must consider the timing aspect. Could we really throw a 15 Yard comeback here? Would have to think most likely not.

"And for my Next Trick…"

| Set: | Spread Gun T | Team: | Medina |
|---|---|---|---|
| Play: | Hook & Ladder | Scheme: | Trick Play |

**Coaches Corner**

Timing, Timing, Timing. When involving s "Special" package like a trick play. Put 5-10 minutes aside for practice to help your RBs understand the patience of this play.

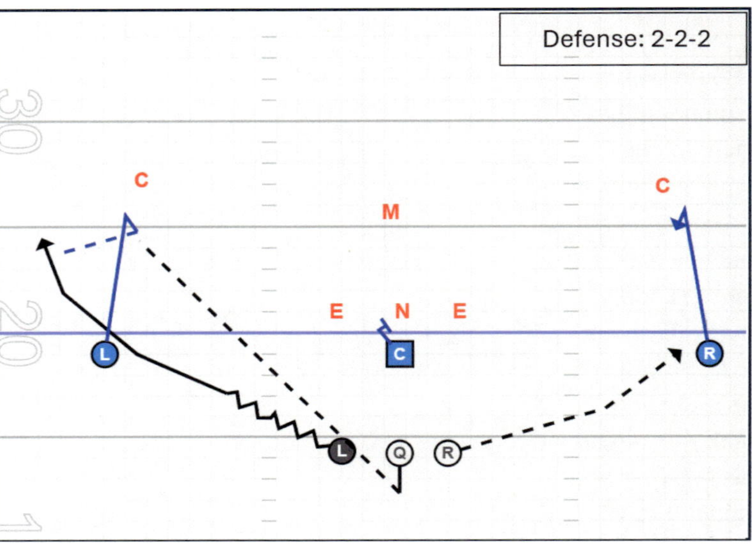


| C: | On (Hook/Seal) | QB: | Snap – Throw to Hitch |
|---|---|---|---|
| LWR: | 5 Yard Hitch – Catch & Pitch | LHB: | 2 Second Delay – Time up pitch w/WR |
| RWR: | 5 Yard Hitch | RHB: | Wheel Route |

*The Clipboard*

I couldn't resist adding in a Trick play! Even though this is something that you won't consider in your base offensive install, doesn't mean it's not great to carry! Taking the easy grass on a hitch is always something you want in pro spread style of offense. But what can be common is CB's being aggressive at the point of the catch.

# The Behind the Back Handoff

| Set: | Pro Gun | Team: | Allen Academy |
|---|---|---|---|
| Play: | Handoff - Sweep | Scheme: | Zone |

**Coaches Corner**

One of the most impressive things about Allen is that even though they've never had more then 12 kids on their roster every year, they still went up-tempo on offense, averaging about 18 seconds per snap.

Defense: 3-3

| C: | On (Hook/Seal) | QB: | Hold ball behind ball – 2nd Level |
|---|---|---|---|
| LWR: | Stalk Block | FB: | Hook/Seal PSDE |
| # 2 WR: | Stalk Block | RB: | Be patient behind QB – Read his block |

*The Clipboard*

This diagram does not do this play enough justice! (Highly recommend **watching the clip** to fully understand this play). Since Allen Academy mostly always offset their RB at a 1x1 yard relationship with the QB. They invented a neat way to run sweep opposite of the RB. Instead of pitching the ball to the RB, the QB will stick the ball behind his back and have the RB literally take the ball from his hands! If you like "pro-gun" sets like Allen's, this would be a great addition to your offense.

| Set: | Diamond Twins | Team: | Hermleigh |
|---|---|---|---|
| Play: | Smash | Scheme: | Sweep Read |

**Coaches Corner**

**Spread = Numbers**. If you've designed a pass concept, always go through the spread checklist: **Numbers, Leverage, Matchups.**

Defense: 3-2-1

| C: | Seam/Pipe | SB: | Progression: Corner – Hitch - Run |
|---|---|---|---|
| LWR: | 5 Yard Hitch | LUB: | Kickout or Hook/Seal PSDE |
| #2 WR: | 8-10 Yard Corner | RUB: | Snap – Pitch – Seal Backside |

*The Clipboard*

Typically, it's odd to see shorter routes like hitches in second exchange spread sets as the timing is hard to get that throw off. But the main reasoning for this concept is to try and **HOLD** the CB and horizontally stretch the 1-High safety between the corner route & center's seam route.

**Note:** It's important to teach your center to try and get eyes on the safety and BEND his route more inside - To get away from the outside leverage of the CB (Or just have him curl).

# Watch me Whip

## *Coaches Corner*

Now considered the 7th highest scoring game in 6-man football history. In their first-round playoff game, Robert Lee & Westbrook combined for 226 Points.

| **Set:** | Diamond Twins | **Team:** | Robert Lee |
|---|---|---|---|
| **Play:** | Whip/Post | **Scheme:** | T.B.O |

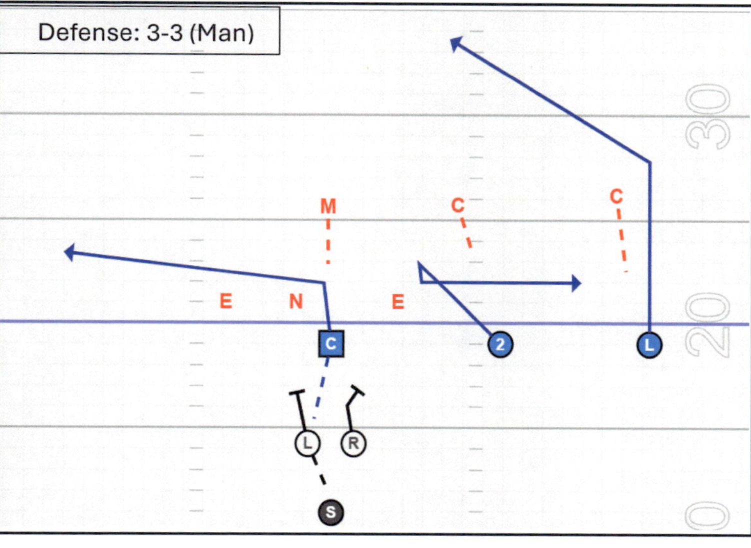


| **C:** | Slant/Flat | **SB:** | Progression: Whip - Post |
|---|---|---|---|
| **RWR:** | 7-8 Yard Post | **LUB:** | Snap – Pitch – Pass Pro Left |
| **#2 WR:** | 3 Step Whip Route | **RUB:** | Pass Pro Right |

*The Clipboard*

Man Beaters = When carrying a series of pass concepts, it's important to remember that you will need to build concepts tailored towards beating man to man defenses. What works well for Robert Lee here, is creating a High-Low situation where the SB can have a simple 2 route progression that hit different areas of the field.

## 2-Man Concept's

| **Set:** | Pro | **Team:** | Emery Weiner |
|---|---|---|---|
| **Play:** | Post/Cross | **Scheme:** | T.B.O |

### *Coaches Corner*

Something unknown about Emery Weiner is that almost every year they start at least 2+ athletes who have never played football before and always have great success.

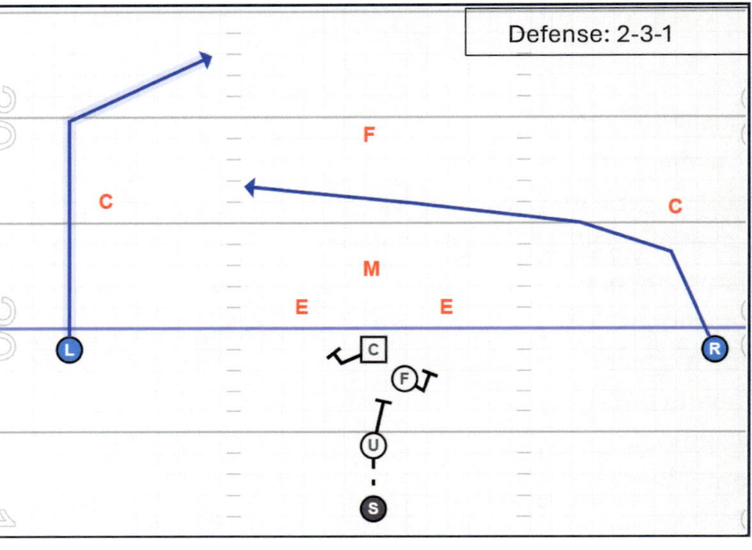


| **C:** | Pass Pro Left | **SB:** | Progression: Post – Cross - Run |
|---|---|---|---|
| **LWR:** | 10-12 Yard Post | **FB:** | Pass Pro Right |
| **RWR:** | 5-7 Yard Cross | **UB:** | Pitch – Pass Pro Both A Gap's |

### *The Clipboard*

A popular defense seen against second exchange types of offenses is a Cover 3 zone (1 High Safety). Especially if the defense trust their LB & Ends to handle any "Dump's" to up-backs. A common thought may be that you must use 3 or 4 routes to try and attack this defense. But that is not case! With the ability to use max protection, if you have deep middle attacking routes, the CBs typically hesitate whether to follow these "in-breaking" routes.

| Set: | Diamond | Team: | Oakwood |
|---|---|---|---|
| Play: | Pump Fake Screen | Scheme: | P.A Screen |

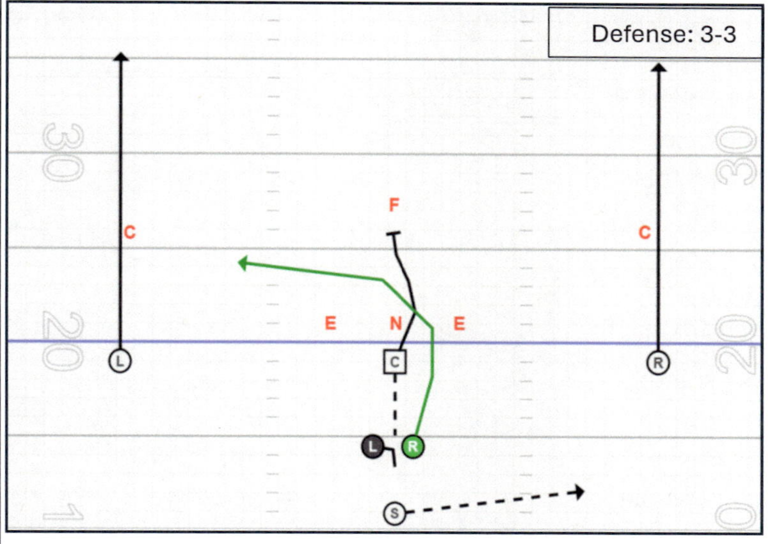


**Coaches Corner**

**Take advantage =** When facing "Odd"/3 Man fronts = If this defense is playing over aggressive – Use your up-backs as a way to slip behind this front.

| C: | 2nd Level | SB: | Sell Sweep |
|---|---|---|---|
| LWR: | M.O.R Fade | LUB: | "Pump Fake" Sweep – Screen to RUB |
| RWR: | M.O.R Fade | RUB: | Delay by 2 count – Dump into flats backside |

*The Clipboard*

**ALWAYS** include your dump game as an extension of your run game. What's important to remember is that usually there is a LB waiting to "hunt down" that dump you are looking to throw. What I love in this design is that by sucking all 3 "D-lineman" past the LOS, we can use the Center as a way to take care of that "spying" linebacker.

## Slipping Through the Cracks

### Coaches Corner

Remember to teach any Crack Block to "Sit and catch" the defender and not "attack" him immediately. The reason for this to avoid any possible "blocking in the back" flags.

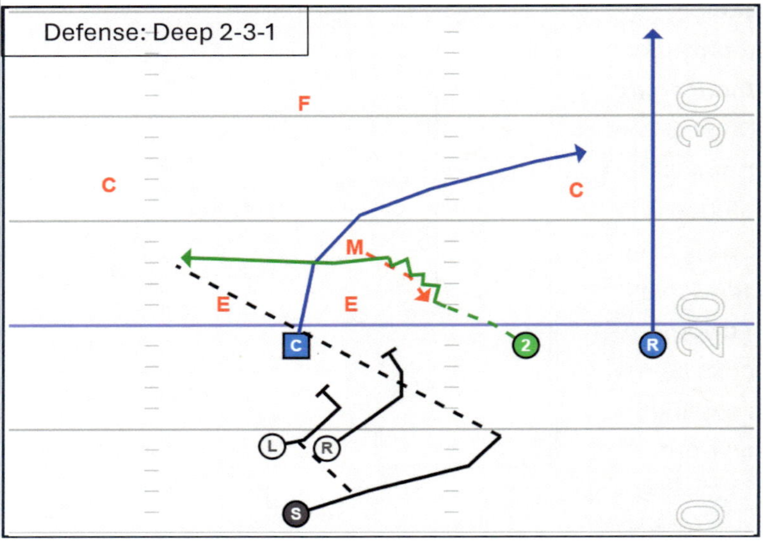

| Set: | Diamond Twins | Team: | Richland Springs |
|---|---|---|---|
| Play: | Sweep – Crack throwback | Scheme: | Throwback |

Defense: Deep 2-3-1

| C: | 8-10 yd. Cross | SB: | Sweep – Throwback to #2 |
|---|---|---|---|
| #2 WR: | Crack Mike – Slip into Drag | LUB: | Snap – Pitch – Seal BSDE |
| RWR: | M.O.R Fade | RUB: | Seal PSDE |

*The Clipboard*

Although ending in a incomplete pass, we see a very good idea of a compliment to "Sweep RPO's." If you have any kind of crack rules or use it as a tag, slipping your crack blocker backside is a great idea! In general, pay attention to how the backside defenders react to "Fast flow" plays (Sweep). If you get a rotation going towards you – Think about having a backside tag available.

## Rock, Paper…

**Coaches Corner**

When designing a pass concept. Focus on putting one defender in stress. Either to vertically or horizontally stretch him. (Like the PSCB here).

| **Set:** | Ruby | **Team:** | O'Donell |
|---|---|---|---|
| **Play:** | Scissors | **Scheme:** | Play Action |

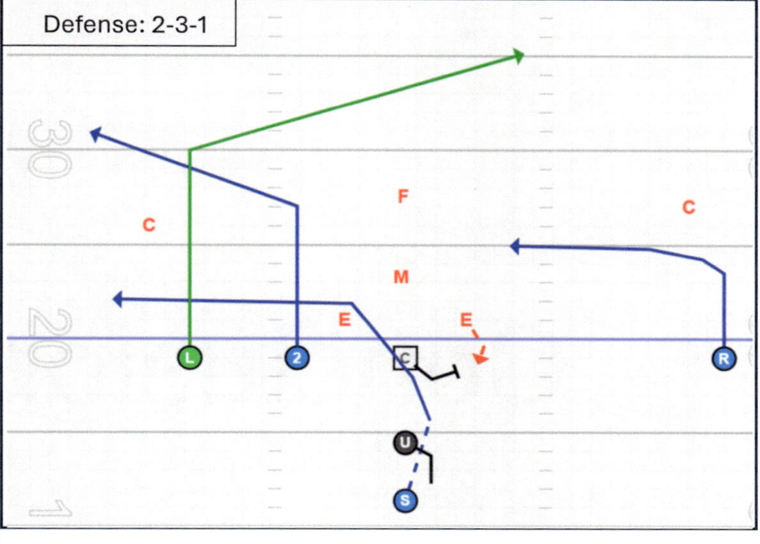


| **C:** | Pass Pro Right | **SB:** | Fake Handoff – Flat Left |
|---|---|---|---|
| **LWR:** | 10-12 Yard Post | **UB:** | Progression: Post – Corner – Flat/In |
| **RWR:** | 5 Yard In | **#2 WR:** | 7-8 Yard Corner |

*The Clipboard*

A Play Action in a spread set? As crazy as this may look, there may be a place for this. Especially since in the clip attached, we see BOTH the Mike & Free safety "bite" on the fake to the Spread Back. The idea of a "scissors" concept is to attack a 1-high coverage anyways, but by putting this safety in even more of a bind by worrying about his run fit responsibility, this help possibly opened the post even more.

# Conclusion

# Teams Used in this Book

*School Map*

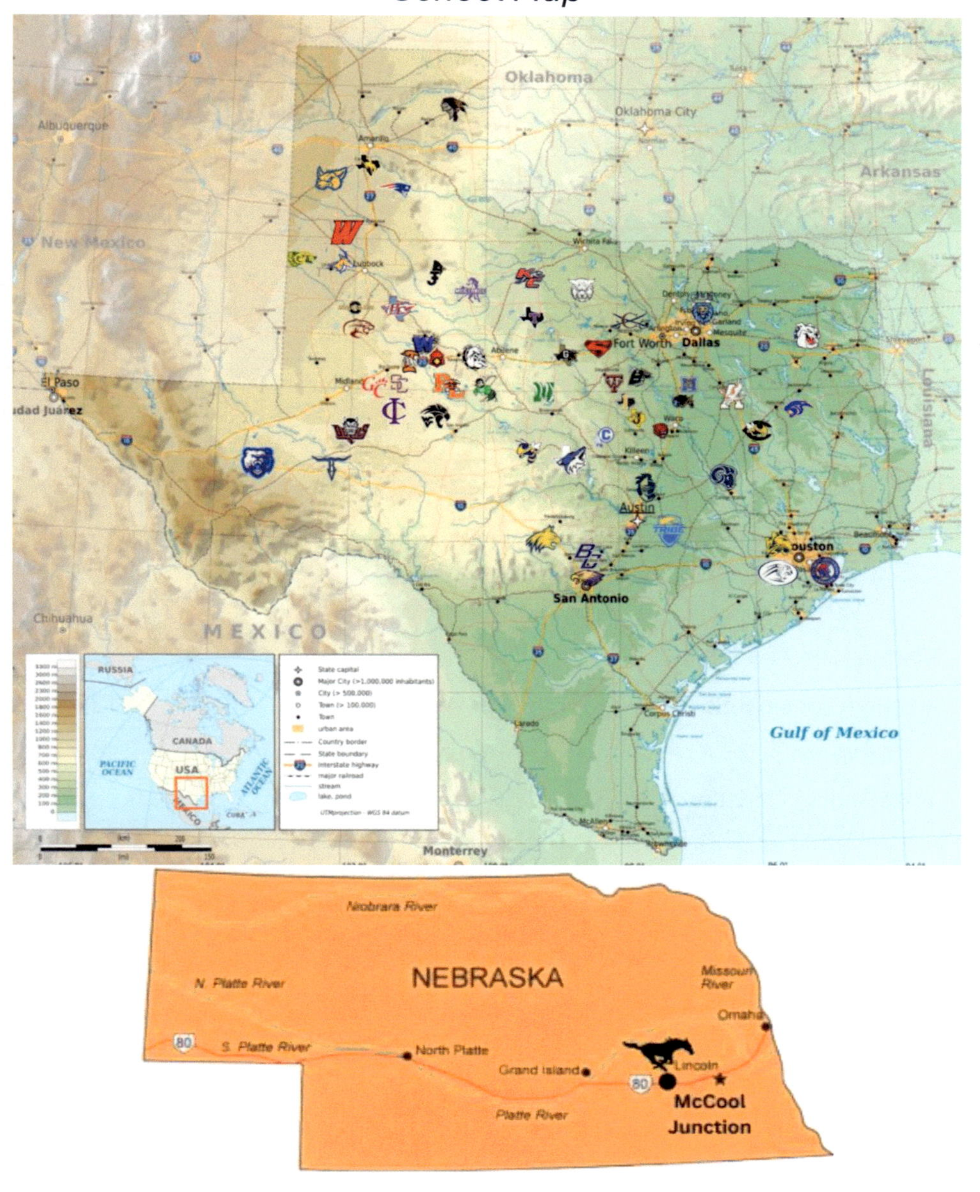

| School | City | H.S Population |
|---|---|---|
| Abbott | Abbott, Texas | 76 |
| Allen Academy | Bryan, Texas | 86 |
| Avalon | Avalon, Texas | 100 |
| Balmorhea | Balmorhea, Texas | 58 |
| Benjamin | Benjamin, Texas | 45 |
| Blackwell | Blackwell, Texas | 55 |
| Blum | Blum, Texas | 96 |
| Borden County | Gail, Texas | 81 |
| Bracken Christian School | Bulverde, Texas | 93 |
| Buena Vista | Imperial, Texas | 93 |
| Cherokee | Cherokee, Texas | 46 |
| Christian School at Castle Hills | Castle Hills, Texas | 156 |
| Coolidge | Coolidge, Texas | 79 |
| Coram Deo Academy | Plano, Texas | 144 |
| Covenant Classical School | Fort Worth, Texas | 128 |
| Emery Weiner | Houston, Texas | 348 |
| First Baptist Christian Academy | Pasadena, Texas | 159 |
| Garden City | Garden City, Texas | 98 |
| Gordon | Gordon, Texas | 75 |
| Happy | Happy, Texas | 91 |
| Hermleigh | Hermleigh, Texas | 77 |
| Hill Country Christian | Austin, Texas | 209 |
| Ira | Ira, Texas | 68 |

| Iredell | Iredell, Texas | 48 |
|---|---|---|
| Irion County | Mertzon, Texas | 87 |
| Jayton | Jayton, Texas | 53 |
| Jonesboro | Jonesboro, Texas | 94 |
| Klondike | Lamesa, Texas | 59 |
| Knox City | Knox City, Texas | 68 |
| Loraine | Loraine, Texas | 44 |
| May | May, Texas | 96 |
| McCool Junction | McCool Junction, Nebraska | 60 |
| Medina | Medina, Texas | 73 |
| Miami | Miami, Texas | 60 |
| Milford | Milford, Texas | 86 |
| Nazareth | Nazareth, Texas | 74 |
| Newcastle | Newcastle, Texas | 77 |
| O'Donell | O'Donnell, Texas | 96 |
| Oakwood | Oakwood, Texas | 55 |
| Oglesby | Oglesby, Texas | 57 |
| Rankin | Rankin, Texas | 78 |
| Richland Springs | Richland Springs, Texas | 57 |
| Robert Lee | Robert Lee, Texas | 80 |
| Rochelle | Rochelle, Texas | 52 |
| Springlake-Earth | Earth, Texas | 101 |
| Sterling City | Sterling City, Texas | 136 (Now 11-man) |
| Strawn | Strawn, Texas | 49 |
| Three-Way | Stephenville, Texas | 43 |

| | | |
|---|---|---|
| Throckmorton | Throckmorton, Texas | 46 |
| Tribe Homeschool | Bastrop, Texas | N/A |
| Turley-Valley | Turkey, Texas | 67 |
| Union Hill | Gilmer, Texas | 96 |
| Water Valley | Water Valley, Texas | 93 |
| Westbrook | Westbrook, Texas | 91 |
| Westbury Christian | Houston, Texas | 145 |
| Whiteface | Whiteface, Texas | 108 (2A) |
| Whitharral | Whitharral, Texas | 50 |

Population numbers were taken from;

University Interscholastic League. (n.d.). *2024–2026 conference alignments: Alphabetical listing by school name*. https://www.uiltexas.org/files/alignments/All_post_alpha_by_conf.pdf

*Texas Association of Private and Parochial Schools. (n.d.).* 2024–2026 alignment landing page. *https://tapps.biz/2024-26-alignment-landing-page/*

Nebraska School Activities Association. (2023). *2023–2024 NSAA enrollment figures*. https://nsaa static.s3.amazonaws.com/textfile/about/2324enroll.pdf

# More 6-Man Resources

## Sixmanfootball.com

THE website of 6-man football. Packed with many resources, live scoreboards on gameday and forums/discussion boards based around all things 6-man.

## Texas 1A Fan

Another great website resource for 6-man football but also all things UIL-1A sports! If you ever are curious about listening to a 6-man game live on the radio, Texas 1A will broadcast many games throughout the season and they even host a podcast!

## Coach Bradley Tarpey

Coach Tarpey post digital 6-man contact multiple times a week on his Twitter/X account. He has also made one of the first 6-man courses on Coachtube.com about the spread defense we run here at FBCA.

To all the Men and Woman who work in this small community of Six-Man Football, the game we all love. To the "Do it all" teachers & A.Ds. You are appreciated and thank you for keeping this beautiful game going.

-Coach Rob